This

A Year in Cricklewood

next year

in ?

Happy New Year

from Pam & David

A Year in Cricklewood

Alan Coren

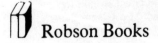 Robson Books

For Rosemary and Alban

First published in Great Britain in 1991 by Robson Books Ltd,
Bolsover House, 5–6 Clipstone Street, London W1P 7EB
This Robson paperback edition first published 1992

British Library Cataloguing in Publication Data
  **A catalogue record for this book is available from the
  British Library.**

  ISBN 0 86051 760 8 (cased)
  ISBN 0 86051 837 X (pbk)

Printed and bound in Great Britain by
WBC Ltd., Bridgend, Mid-Glamorgan.

JUNE

Hard Cheese

Tuesday was a really bad day. I could concentrate on nothing. You must know how it is when, every time a plane goes over, you look up, in case it is your cheese flying to Montevideo. You would not be able to see it, even if it were, but that makes no difference. Pratt & Whitney rattle your mullions, you break off from what you are doing, you peer out, you see a vapour trail, and you think: *is that my Reblochon?*

Whereafter, and for some time, you can concentrate on little else.

It had all begun the night before, at Nice airport. I had been looking forward to buckling myself into my snug little 757 for a 20.50 departure, but this was not to be. For it was not only Bank Holiday Monday, it was also Monaco Grand Prix weekend, a double-header which no self-respecting French air-traffic militant could ignore; and in consequence the place seethed with drunks who should by now have been sleeping it off on their own sofas instead of crawling around the departure lounge on all fours, gabbling about Mansell's clapped-out gearbox and wondering whether there was time for another quick one.

There was. We did not get off until 22.40; and what we got off in, furthermore, was not a 757 but a 747, to enable the strike-struck backlog to be cleared up in one fell flight. The result was that 500 wrecks arrived at Heathrow two hours late and looked at the three cab-drivers who hadn't yet decided to sod this for a game of soldiers. In the queue which subsequently formed, I was perhaps 484th; it was thus 2am when the moment came for me to heft into the cab the two suitcases which I had so far only nudged forward with my foot, and discover that the smaller was far lighter than it should have been.

I opened it. It had a white tuxedo in it. I had not checked in a white tuxedo. I had checked in 10kg of Reblochon, St Hectaire, Vieux Pané, Camembert, and a big block of Bleu d'Auvergne so wondrously marbled that, had you invited Michelangelo over for dinner, he would have had a chisel on it before you could get the cellophane off the water-biscuits.

But where was it now? I snatched up both cases and ran back into the terminal. There was a desk. There was a girl. But there was no suitcase identical to the one I was jabbering about. There was no suitcase at all. All the luggage from flight BA 2343 had been claimed. Some of it, moreover, by passengers connecting with international departures. Even as I spoke, an engine throttled up for take-off. Could be the cheese, en route for Zaire.

I left the small suitcase, and took a piece of paper which said "Details of your missing luggage have been entered into a world-wide baggage-tracing computer system" (the heart sank) "and, in the unlikely event you have not been reunited with your luggage within 24 hours, ring . . ."

I almost wept at "reunited". I had seen a lot of movies like that. True, they had not involved men and suitcases running towards one another in slow motion, weeping, while Henri Mancini brought up the string section, but the principle was not dissimilar. This, however, was the other one. This was the one about the suitcase flying out to a new life

8

with someone else while the camera pulled slowly back on the lonely figure standing on the tarmac.

I got in at 3am, but I couldn't sleep. I kept thinking about the other man. Was some red-eyed Formula One buff even now fending off the left jab of a waiting spouse who had been expecting a jeroboam of Chanel No 5, not 20lb of listeria? And what about the white tux? Did it bespeak an invitation to some Grand Ball in, say, Rio, and, if so, what would come over him as he snapped the locks? Still, if it was fancy-dress, he could always hang the cheeses round him and go as a milk-subsidy. Might pull the big prize. Might win a set of luggage.

So Tuesday was a bad day. But Wednesday was better. Wednesday, the doorbell rang. It was a BA courier. You have to hand it to British Airways, especially if they've just handed it to you.

The cheese was all there, but I haven't tried it yet. I keep hearing my mother's voice saying don't eat that, you never know where it's been.

Snake in the Grass

Let none sneer at Mrs Dorothy Frances Gurney. Any literatrice spry enough to spot the fortune to be made by including sundial rights in her contract deserves our special respect, never mind the fact that so commending yourself to your readers that millions of them are prepared to commission a truck to carry your poetry home and two strong men to erect same in rockery clearly bespeaks a talent which has fingered the public pulse like very few. Her works will stand, albeit in many cases slightly askew, long after those of tonier scribblers have crumbled to dust on neglected shelves. That is one of the things about granite.

Nevertheless, I beg leave to dispute her declaration that one is nearer God's heart in a garden than anywhere else on earth. That you have the kiss of the sun for pardon and the song of the birds for mirth, I shall not quarrel with, for poets are a breed apart, and if they are so innocent that a sunbeam can absolve their guilts and a blackbird have them rolling helpless in the shrubbery, it is not for the rest of us to wonder whether they would not be even happier in a rubber room. When, however, Dorothy Frances induces, in her ringing pay-off, the general from the personal, she lays herself open to argument.

For it would have to be a very peculiar God indeed to whose heart nothing than a garden brought one nearer. What one is nearest to in a garden is chaos, frustration, despair, disease, decay, and the wholesale slaughter of as many of God's creatures as one can get a nozzle over. What one is nearest to is God's anger with the first gardener for ignoring what it said on the packet. Clearly, God now deploys the garden in constant reminder of man's first disobedience.

Which is why what Mrs Gurney should have written was that one was nearer God's heart in a garden *centre*. It may be that the canny old bird figured that the cost of chiselling an extra word on a bird-bath might make punters think twice, it may simply be that, like most poets, she believed that scansion should take priority over mere truth, but whatever the reason, she has left it to me to mop up after her.

For what a garden centre is about is redemption: it is about renewal, rededication, and man's struggle towards perfectibility. Dig up the old, fork in the new. All those uncontaminated seeds, all those immaculately conceived bedders, all those spotless new implements and kinkless hoses and unwarped trellises! Unrotted stakes! Wall-nails with points! Sprinklers that actually go round! What is this but man's God-given chance to make a fresh start?

And Granville Garden Centre is Cricklewood's paragon. When other helpers fail, and comforts flee, it takes but a moment for the helpless to canter round there, bury their faces in the pinnies of God's kindly acolytes, weepily confess that change and decay in all around they see, and get instantly sorted out. The beacon above the signboard of its untainted premises shines like a good deed in a naughty world.

Or shone.

Did you guess? Did you feel the apocalyptic descant in this morning's witterings? Did it occur to you that yesterday I might have rushed to Granville's, only to be turned away?

An ancient rose-bush had finally succumbed. I bit the lip, and dug it up. I stared at the hole. I needed a new Korresia Floribunda, and I needed it now. I hurtled to Granville. I need a rose-bush, I cried. The acolyte shook his head. They're filming in the rose section, he said. I peered. Lights, lenses, mike-booms teetered among the thorns. Oh, I said, a gardening programme, oh that's all right then, it's about time Granville got its rightful place on the horticultural map, I can wait, they won't take long. I know these low-budget jobs.

They'll be here all day, he said. It is not a gardening programme, it is a film about terrorists, they are smuggling Semtex by planting it in rose-tubs, I'd come back tomorrow if I were you. I looked at him. He looked away. They're paying us good money, he said.

Et tu, Granville? The director called for silence; as it fell, did I only imagine the dreadful susurration of a serpent slithering down a tree?

A Sense of Loss

The Kenyan state of emergency notwithstanding, I spent the autumn of 1953 doing the foxtrot. Also waltz and quickstep. Despite the best efforts of the Mau Mau to interfere, my lissom partner and I passed every Friday evening locked in romantic ensemble, dancing across the polished parquet of our elegant Palmers Green trysting-place, and murmuring into one another's ears such little nonsenses as dancers do.

Which, by the by, is how I first met Humphrey Lyttelton and Wally Fawkes; two brilliant polymaths whom, years later, I was to employ in their other capacities, and so happily that nobody seeing us together would ever have realized that one of them had once told me what he proposed to do with his clarinet if I ever again interrupted a performance of Trog's Blues, nor that the other had ribaldly added that it was the duty of the brass to accompany the woodwind, wherever it chose to blow. I met them because this lurid offer was made in the rehearsal chamber directly above our little ballroom, connected to it by a staircase up which my partner had just dispatched me.

"You tell them buggers we can't hear ourselves dance," my partner had said. "You inform 'em there is nothing in the book says musicians has to bang their feet on the floor all the bloody time."

No sooner had I scuttled down again than the band struck up its revenge. King Porter Stomp rattled the casements.

Plaster settled on our waltzing shoulders, like eau-de-Nil scurf. My partner said "right", lifted the Dansette arm from the disc, and dashed out. Suddenly, remarkably, the noise above my head faded to a tinny bleat.

"What did you say?" I inquired, as, blissfully reunited, we floated through Charmaine.

"Nothing," said my partner, reversing sleekly, "I just give 'em a look."

It reflects naught upon the courage of jazzers that one look had been enough. My partner was built like a Martello tower. Against the neckless head, a busy life had flattened nose and ears alike, while fists of hirsute rock and a tell-tale way of easing his shoulders suggested that Mr Ronga considered it even more blessed to give than to receive.

He had been a sergeant in the Parachute Regiment; but, despite his heroic service to King and country, neither would let him kill anybody after VJ day, so he chucked in the beret and set himself up as a dance instructor. My mother found him in *The Palmers Green Gazette*. I was 15, and it was time I learned to dance. I would thank her one day.

I enrolled for the bronze medal course. If successful, I might be allowed to enrol in the silver, and learn the tango. Not the rumba. You had to have a gold medal to do the rumba in public. If you attempted the rumba without a gold medal, Edmundo Ros would send the boys round.

In a moment, you will find out why I am telling you all this.

When my first lesson was over, my partner shook his huge head and told me I should have to buck my ideas up, due to where, any day now, it was on the cards the Paras would be asked to go and sort out Kenya, in which case he might very likely rejoin. Time was of the wossname. In consequence, we used only three records, all by Victor Sylvester, so that I could gear my movements by rote to every familiar chord. Furthermore, Mr Ronga would see to it that my feet would not betray me by touching the ground. Biceps like cricket balls would carry me through. I can feel them still.

The inspector arrived the week before Christmas. He had

a briefcase. He took three records out of it. I heard, cheek to cheek, my partner's teeth grind. "The bastard has brought his own music!" he muttered. He dropped me, shimmied across to the inspector, glanced at his labels. "Joe Loss?" he said. "Joe Loss? We don't do Joe Loss here. We do Victor Sylvester."

The inspector opened his mouth; but shut it again. My partner had given him a look. Not only did I get strict tempo, I also got the medal. I am telling you all this because, just as I was about to tell you something else, I heard that Joe Loss had died, and it all came back.

Garden Pests

We physicists know a thing or two about the relationship between heat and friction. The thing I know is that there is a relationship. Had I not given up physics at 14, I should probably have found out what the other thing was, but there you are, you cannot be everywhere at once.

Anyhow, if God had wanted us to know everything, he would not have given us the British educational system. Free will is the Almighty's way, and who am I to argue with that? Especially since I gave up divinity the same term. Offered the choices, I shrewdly guessed that my life would be better served by an ability to decline *amo* and list the principal exports of the Gold Coast, and I have not been proved wrong.

This does not prevent me from taking as today's text the

observation that heat produces friction. I have of course heard that there is a body of opinion which holds the opposite view, but that is no more than you would expect from mere theorists. They ought to get out and about a bit. And what they ought to get out and about to is more lunchtime drinks parties, now that the ozone has, as I understand it, gone through the greenhouse layer, and there's more to come, say the weathermen.

For we have suddenly become a race which drinks *al fresco*. We have people over at noon, and we usher them towards lawn and flagstone, and we fill their right hands, and they amble about among shrub and tub, and the sun thrums down upon them, and they chat and chortle happily enough, and all is more or less as it was in the blissful days before it was 82° and still rising. And then the friction enters the soul.

Do not get ahead of me: I am not about to address that homicidal irritability which comes to lesser breeds when the mercury goes up. These are civilized folk of whom I speak – should the sun-kissed talk turn to, say, Heseltine or Latvia or the Booker Prize, they do not take swings at one another, they do not fumble beneath the sweated seersucker for Colt and life-preserver, they do not roll amid the petunias, their hands locked around one another's throats.

All that happens when the hot weather strikes is that they say things outside which they would never dream of saying inside. The only part, indeed, which the heat plays is to put them where they can do the saying. In the old, cold days of yore, you had people over for summer drinks, and they stared out at the drizzle for a bit, and then they got on with the sluicing and the small talk. What they never, ever, did was criticize their surroundings. They did not say: "Did you realize your carpet has got moth?" Or: "I know a bit about furniture, and that chiffonier is unquestionably fake." Or: "It's time you had that rising damp seen to." Or: "I've sat on a few uncomfortable sofas in my time, but this one takes the bloody biscuit!"

So why should it be that the simple act of shepherding

them out into the sunshine should have the effect of stripping from them all pretence of civility? Why, as you are topping up his glass, should a guest nod downward towards his feet and observe: "Yes, well, you realize of course that the only way to get rid of all this couch-grass is to dig the whole thing up and start again?", the man on his right chuckle and say: "Never mind couch-grass, as far as I am aware couch-grass doesn't fall on you, have you taken a look at that chimney of his, I give it six months, tops" and the man on his left chip in with "Yes, I noticed the chimney when I was looking at his guttering, you ought to have that guttering seen to, half the brackets have rusted off"?

Why do their wives then join you so that one can point out that if you don't do something about the leaf-curl on your eucryphia it'll be dead by tea-time, and another shriek "First things first, have you seen the thrips on his gladdies, you'd think he'd never heard of Malathion!" while the third inquires icily whether you have something to bang her heel back on with, and her husband smirks and says, "I warned you about that path of his, didn't I?"

Forgive me, I only observe this, I cannot explain it. To me, psychology is an even more closed book than physics.

Jam Today

A couple of mornings ago, I was reading a piece in *The Times* on the M25. In both senses. (What a flexible little helpmeet that preposition is!)
To my left lay West Thurrock. To my right – in the curious

16

absence of East Thurrock – lay Purfleet. And before me lay the Dartford Tunnel. Which is to say that before me lay several hundred vehicles, all of them as stationary as the several hundred behind me, and spread across my steering wheel lay *The Times*.

For some time now, print demographers have been earning their crusts by pondering the various socio-cultural explanations for the continuing expansion of the broadsheet market and the continuing diminution of the tabloid one. I shall not bother you with their numerous conclusions, merely remark that in my regular scrutiny of these, in this professional journal and that, I have seen no mention made of the most obvious one: which is that for every mile of new motorway laid, an exponential amount of new daily reading matter, i.e., big fat papers, is required by drivers sitting motionless upon it. Once upon a time, only rail commuters read newspapers, but now the contraflow is true.

Did I read the professional journals of the catering trade, I should doubtless find this argument cheerfully substantiated. I cannot believe that sales of pork pies, thermos flasks and paper napkins have not risen in direct ratio to the laying of multiple carriageways.

I myself rarely leave the house without a wicker hamper, even if my target is no further than Swiss Cottage. Indeed, after I had finished Wednesday's crossword and was left with only wool-gathering to pass the time, it was borne in upon me how travelling was gradually returning to the conditions of *The Pickwick Papers*. What bore it was (a) the fact that my notional route would take me through Rochester, and (b) the reflection that, if I ever arrived there, I might leave my shoes outside the car door to see whether Sam Weller would pop out and polish them while the car and I passed the night in the fast lane. Before I began mulling that, however, I had already gathered a fair amount of the wool spinning out of the article by Nick Nuttall, Our Technology Correspondent. He was reporting the granting by the government of an operating licence to something called Trafficmaster, a title which we might well feel to be a blow

17

to the *amour propre* of Transport Secretary Cecil Parkinson, especially since it is designed to get us out of the fine messes his department continues to get us into.

For Trafficmaster is an electronic scanning system which feeds into a portable gizmo which the driver rents at £1.30 a day so that it can tell him where motorway traffic jams are. He may then avoid them by getting off on to non-motorways. It will initially cover M's 1, 3, 4, 40, 23, 20, 11, and, of course, 25, and will soon be extended to the rest.

Excellent. Astonishing. What a boon. Have motorists not dreamed of some such miracle ever since that first fateful moment when a man walking in front of a car with a red flag suddenly found himself coming to a halt behind a car with another man with a red flag in front of it?

But hardly had this marvellous news sunk in than there flashed above my head something not unlike the phenomenon which diverted St Paul's attention from the traffic jam outside Damascus. The motorway system had been designed and installed, at appalling expense, to solve the problems of traffic-flow on the existing and inadequate roads.

The object of Trafficmaster, as I understand it, is to solve the problems of traffic-flow on the motorways by directing drivers back to the roads from which they had been invited to escape. Since there are now twice as many vehicles in Britain as there were on the day the M1 opened, this process may be likened to decanting a pint into a quart pot, and when it more than doubles to the point of running over the rim, putting it back in the pint pot again.

I am not, you understand, complaining. If traffic-jams are poised to become twice as big, it can only be good news for good newspapers.

Good God, That's Never the Time?

Fifty-two? No age, they said. Fifty-two? *These* days? No age! They said it all day Wednesday. Rang up, dropped in, brought presents, popped corks, filled the premises with cheery cards (albeit mainly about impotence and coffins), shouted, through clouds of marzipan crumbs, what Gladstone did at 87, what Picasso did at 83, what Rubinstein did at 88.

Convinced me utterly. Despite what, after 50, has become the annual shock of seeing it written down, I did not feel what 52 sounded as if one should feel like. After tea, I went over to the club and played three sets without dying, and it was one of those good days when the Fate who handles the fortuity portfolio allows the ball to coincide with the racquet more often than not, and you think, *Bring me Ivan! Bring me Boris!*, and you jog home feeling good, despite the little bird trilling beside you to the effect that even if they were to bring you Fred Perry, you'd be going back on a stretcher.

And when what was lowered into the subsequent bath appeared to displace no more water than it had done when its digits were in reverse order, and when its glottis proved still competent to handle *Ol' Man River* without a quiver at either end of the register, and when its teeth stood up to the Extra Hard without the hint of a wobble, and especially when it sloshed on its new skin bracer, tautening each incipient wrinkle to the sleekness of a snare-drum, could it not be forgiven for murmuring to itself: "52? No age!"

19

So I skipped downstairs, and I decanted lunch's dissimilar dregs into a single tumbler with that nonchalance which springs from the conviction that 52 is no age for a liver, either, and I set about tearing wrappers from the rest of my presents with these amazingly youthful fingers I have, and, oh what fun!, someone had given me a video called *1938: A Year To Remember*.

I put it on. It was a compilation of Pathé newsreels. Black and white, of course. No colour newsreels, then. And who is this, stepping out of a piston-engined item at what the commentator, in his jovial cut-glass accent, tells me is an aerodrome? The chap is waving a piece of paper. He has a wing-collar on. He is surrounded by photographers in three-piece suits. They keep removing bulbs from what look like frying-pans. The commentator is very happy. "This is the greatest diplomatic triumph of modern times!" he cries.

And what's this? The scene has changed. "A new giant of the sky is floating into the mist on its maiden flight!" This is September 1938. I am already on strained solids. I am older than the Graf Zeppelin.

Oh, look, here comes sport. Wimbledon finals day. Men leaping about in long trousers. "And so we say farewell to Bunny Austin!" Tonight, it will be Donald Budge leading Helen Wills Moody on to the parquet. What will they murmur, as they waltz decorously at arm's length? That they would be able to go home on the Queen Elizabeth, if only it had been launched? Oh, look, there it is being launched now. Not the QE2, of course. There wasn't anyone to name a QE2 after, yet, except that little girl running about.

That's her father, now, on a beach, surrounded by small boys. He is singing "Ooja! Ooja! Rub A Dub A Dub!" It makes a change from trekking round council estates. "Their majesties go into humble homes!" shrieks the commentator. "This Hoxton house is 12 shillings a week!"

There is a child outside, in a pram. I crane: could it be? Too late, here is Hutton knocking up 364, here is a flying-boat inaugurating the England-Australia run, here is six-year-old Teddy Kennedy opening the Children's Zoo, here is Gracie, singing as we go, here is Englishman Dick Seaman winning the German grand prix in what appears to be a Mercedes soap-box car. Dick has a swastika round his neck.

The End. And, at that exact moment, a Lancaster thrums overhead, rattling the sashes, and I run outside just in time to see it, flanked by a Spitfire and a Hurricane. How nice of Tom King to lay it on, if a little *de trop*. It's not as if I'm 90, or anything, like the Queen Mother.

Just 52. No age, these days. Hardly older than a Lancaster.

JULY

Six Legs Bad, Two Legs Worse

There are no flies on me. So why is one of my ears larger than the other? Were this a decent comic, that intriguing little prolegomenon would be followed by (*Answer: foot of col. 6*), whereupon, having turned the page upside down, the reader would immediately fall about, slapping his thigh and hooting, and repeating the joke to as many neighbours as he could manage before being asked to stand in the corridor. But, sadly for all of us, time has cracked on a bit since Form 4a and life's riddles no longer offer themselves up for quick solutions. This is a serious publication, and even after I have led you through 800 words of verbal wilderness, we shall not catch sight of the promised answer. When we get to the foot of page 27, no good, I am afraid, will come of turning the page around. We shall be none the wiser.

On Saturday morning, the weather took a turn for the better so I went into the garden with a book. Which book doesn't matter, but you ought to know that it didn't smell. I am a great sniffer of books; it is a particular pleasure, and one which ensures, for me at least, that television will never replace great literature; I can thus be sure that the book, on this occasion, was entirely unscented. So was I. I had just showered, I was clean as a whistle, I did not smell of anything at all. Certainly not of rotten plum or midge. All around me, on the other hand, the garden smelt of everything a warm July garden smells of. For anything keen on smelling, I was the last place to go.

As I opened the book, I felt feet on my left ear. I shook my head, gently, and the wasp took off, did a couple of circuits of my head, and landed on my right ear. I was thus forced to conclude that it had not landed in error. It had been on the lookout for an ear.

These days, one does not set about the execution of wasps lightly. Apart from the fact that we are all caring one-world persons now, live and let live, there is the question of even more caring one-world persons walking about in balaclava helmets and Wasp Rights sashes, ready to lob a Molotov cocktail over the fence at the first sound of swatting. I therefore lifted my book to my ear, in the hope that the wasp would walk on to it and could then be carried caringly to somewhere earless.

No bibliophile, it. I could tell this from a sudden sharp pain in the lobe. I leapt, flailed, swore, and sprinted into the house to hold an ice-cube against the ear to reduce the swelling. After a few minutes, I had a big, cold ear. At this point, William Shakespeare murmured "Sweet are the uses of adversity", and I knew what I had to do. If a big throbbing ear was not to be wasted, I should have to find out why I had it. I went to the library.

While the librarian was looking at my ear, I said "Have you got a good book on wasps?" She came back with Burton's *Encyclopaedia of Insects*, Reynold's *Bees and Wasps*, and Daglish's *Name That Insect* (which, if I am any judge of the culture, could well be an ITV celebrity quiz show any day now), and by 3pm, I had vespology under my belt. Were I ever to find myself round a bridge table with Burton, Reynolds and Daglish, my small talk would leave them stunned. I know not only that the queen wasp, unable to make wax, builds her nest from spit and paper, but that, unlike the queen bumblebee, she starts with the roof. There she is fed on chewed-up insects by her sexless daughters, but they do no housework. This is done by the hoverfly, which eats wasp droppings.

I know a lot more stuff like this, but I have room only to tell you that the wasp subsists on midges and nectar, particularly that oozing from rotten fruit, and that all three authorities go to great pains to stress that the wasp is thus a wonderful friend to me. But I am an authority, too, now – especially when it comes to great pain – and what I have been unable to discover is why, if we are neither rotten fruit nor midges, wasps want to walk on our ears, and sting us when we object. On this, Burton, Reynolds and Daglish are silent. They say nothing about wasps and men, except that they are wonderful friends.

Meat and One Veg

Let me immediately say that I have no complaints. I had a corking time. All that happened was that I got blown about a bit, but I'd been ready for that. When he sits down at table beside the woman responsible for the most contentious meals in living memory, the wise man trims for squall. What I was not prepared for was the quarter from which the wind would gust.

On Monday, Foyle's threw a lunch in honour of Frank Muir and *The Oxford Book of Humorous Prose*, a work which these 17 years past has been his *magnum onus*. It is a

Falstaff of a book, immoderately fat, quintessentially English, vulgar and noble by turns, and not only witty in itself but – to judge from the punters reeling about the Grosvenor House premises and helplessly choking on this plum and that – the cause that wit is in other men. There were some 200 of us foregathered to launch it, and a well-oiled slipway we conjointly formed.

I was sitting between Max Jaffa, doyen of fiddlers, and Carla Lane, the great Scouse scriptwriter, neither of them previously known to me. Which direction to turn on such occasions is ever the crux, as indeed it is in life: the choice could change you for ever. It has formed the nub of many a Central European determinist text (moth-eaten man and dog arrive at deserted crossroads, man flips coin, man goes one way, dog the other, you know the sort of thing), but it is no whit less fraught in Park Lane.

Had I plumped for my left-hand option, who knows what might not have transpired? For, as we sat down, the first thing Max Jaffa said to me was that he had spent his pre-war years in Cricklewood. I sensed a door rolling back upon a treasure-house, but before I could grab my gunny sack and delve, I felt I should at least turn to my right and introduce myself to the inventor of *Bread*. It was a shock: expecting the creator of the battling Boswells to have tattooed forearms and wooden dentures, I was astonished to find an elegant slip of a girl staring mournfully at her fillet of smoked trout, and sighing.

"Yes, it's infuriating when they serve it without the head, isn't it?" I said, for, faced with a pretty woman, I can be a silver-tongued bastard. "I like poking about for the brain, don't you?"

"I am a vegetarian," she replied. "I know how fish die. Last week, I walked out of my favourite restaurant because they'd put frogs' legs on the menu. They just throw the live bodies in the bin, you know."

She paused, to allow a waiter to replace her trout with a melon. I had a somewhat listless go at my fillet, while Carla told me how they trapped mink. Safe enough ground: I never eat mink. But there was turkey next. I knew that, because the waiter came and asked if Carla wanted turkey, and she went white. Just bring the vegetables, she said.

Mine came. You would never know it was turkey. It was a breaded cutlet, not unlike a giant cornflake. I can probably eat this without inviting too much opprobrium, I thought, when Carla murmured: "I save pigeons."

"Ah," I quipped. Hardly surprising Frank put me in his book and dropped Oscar Wilde.

"I go out at night in the car, looking, and if I find one lying about, I bring him home and nurse him. I found one recently with a twisted neck. All he could do was walk round in circles."

I put down my fork.

"When it got better, it wouldn't fly away. I tried to persuade it to, but it hopped on to my shoulder."

Lucky it wasn't a turkey, I thought. I did not, of course, say so. I just shoved my cutlet about a bit, because, having finished her veg, Carla was free to look at me. She would see me slicing up the corpse. She would see it vanishing through a hole in my face. I put down my knife.

Which at least gave us plenty of opportunity to chat. Vivisection, mad cow disease, the tragedy of the mudworm, the horror of leather; all that and more. As I say, a corking time. After all, I can eat any day.

I might phone Max Jaffa, soon. See if he fancies a spot of lunch.

Numbers Racket

Y you will, of course, remember the opening sequence of *A Matter of Life and Death*. How could you not? It was a seminal moment in the history of telecommunications. No one who cares about phones could ever forget it. I wonder sometimes whether even Powell and Pressburger realized the magnitude of what they had stumbled upon: they probably thought they were just making a film about life and death.

The credits fade to reveal David Niven, piloting his bomber back from Germany. Things are not good. The Germans have taken exception to being assaulted by an actor in a cardboard Lancaster, and set fire to it. Furthermore, Niven has suffered a nasty head wound, as the result of heavy ketchup over the Ruhr. He is not going to make it back. We know this from his smile. It is the smile of a man whose director has just suggested that he should appear to have met with Triumph and Disaster and to be treating those two impostors just the same, though not for much longer.

It is at this point that he begins to trawl the ether, seeking some sympathetic voice to say pip-pip to. But nothing negotiates the RT save static – until, suddenly, a girl's voice crackles. It is Kim Hunter, a toothsome American wireless operator: as they chat, her bee-stung mouth trembles, her velvet eyes brim, and, even though the skipper has never seen her and can have no inkling that Miss Hunter is a little stunner, they fall in love. It is her voice which enraptures him. It is the last thing he hears as he goes into his terminal plummet.

What follows is two hours of fey tosh, with Niven dangling in limbo while supernal advocates dispute whether he is alive or dead, until he is duly redeemed by the love of the operator and allowed to resurrect. But none of that mattered. I knew this even at the age of 10, when I tottered, blinking, from the Southgate Odeon. What mattered was the core-truth; which was that you never knew who you might run into at the telephone exchange.

For four decades, that notion of limitless possibility sustained me. Nor – which has not always been the case with other dreams – did disillusion lie in wait for it with a sockful of sand. I have had some delightful natters, oft in the stilly night, with operators; many a chat, flirtatious, comical, subversive, has warmed the wires between us. Could be directory enquiries, who, as their wet thumb flicked the pages, would rabbit revealingly of this and that; could be some reverse-chargehand answering with a mouthful of pork pie, and before you knew it you were into an engaging exchange about nocturnal indulgence; could be just one of those who happened to be giggling as they connected, and you said what's the joke, and she said we're having a bit of a laugh down here, Denise is getting married Wednesday to this bloke with a peculiar walk, and from there it was but a short step to intimate conspiracies.

It's all over now. There is not a human being left at the nation's switchboards, save the handful required to press the buttons which activate BT's androids. Any enquiry is answered by a computerized thing. The thing says "sorry, the number you want is ex-directory", or "sorry, the number you want is unobtainable", or "the cellphone subscriber you have dialled is away from his instrument at this time". Last evening, after a thing gave me a number, I dialled it, and another thing said: "You have been answered by a fax-link. Please fax now, or hold for a telephone connection." It then played most of *Eine Kleine Nachtmusik* before putting me through to a third thing which said: "Sorry, the number has been changed to . . ."

This is a bad business. In the Next Lot, when I am limping home with the tailplane shot away and my chute in tatters, what shall I hear when I punch the plaintive button? "Sorry, this number has been changed to a fax-link and the subscriber is away from the instrument at this time, but if you would care to leave your name and code and number after the *Toccata and Fugue*, we shall try to get back to you as soon as . . ."

Avon Calling

I have a homunculus on my right buttock. When I move one way, he smiles; another, and he grows glum. Grave and gay by turns, as he himself put it when he was a touch more alive than he is now.

This is a bit bloody peculiar, you will be saying. You do not know the half of it. Jumping to the conclusion that I am tattooed will get you nowhere; my fair flesh is virgin to the buzzing needle. I have always held the view that life is complicated enough as it is without having a lost lover's *embonpoint* ineradicably going up and down every time you flex a pectoral. That said, the little fellow in my hip pocket is very nearly as permanent a fixture: I dare not go far without him.

He arrived yesterday, from Lloyds Bank, wrapped in a letter. *We enclose a replacement cheque card for your use*, said the letter, *please sign the card immediately*. It was the work of a moment to do this, and it would have been the work of another to slip the new card into my wallet had I not, as I did so, noticed a fuzzy little face in the corner of it. Hallo, I said, a breakthrough. What a good idea, sticking the cardholder's face on a card, that is one in the eye for mugger and pickpocket. And I put my glasses on to check the likeness.

It was a bloke with a beard. As I turned the tiny hologram, his expression changed several times, but it never became mine. Here we go, I said – as I have said so often when colliding with a technological glitch – they have sent me someone else's card. Is it not amazing, I said to the manikin, that, in this day and age, we can put a man on the moon, but we cannot guarantee that it will be the right man?

I uncrumpled the binned letter. *If the card is lost*, it said, *please inform the Chief Inspector, Lloyds Bank plc, 071-626 1500.*

"You have got the name right," I informed Cashplod, "but the picture is not of me."

"It is not supposed to be of you. It is William Shakespeare."

I looked again. It was a photograph.

"How did you get a photograph of Shakespeare?" I inquired.

"It is an actor," said the Chief Inspector, "dressed up."

"All right," I said, because I am a reasonable man. "I can accept the how. What about the why? Why is there a hologram of William Shakespeare on my cheque guarantee card?"

"Not my department," said the Chief Inspector. "I suggest you speak to Jim Parsons. He handles corporate communications at APACS."

"APACS?"

He sighed. "The Association for Payment Clearing Services," he said.

"Hello, Jim," I said, after a bit, and popped the question.

"We call it the Bard Card," said Jim. "It facilitates recognition."

"Only of Shakespeare," I said. "I can see where if Shakespeare fetched up at the Tesco's till they would be more than happy to accept his cheque. Mind you, that said, it does occur to me that he never signed his name the same way twice. It is quite possible that if he put Shagsper, your Chief Inspector would have his glove on the Bard's collar before he'd got his trolley half way to the Volvo."

I was losing Jim. You can sense things like that.

"It is not about identifying the cardholder," said Jim, a mite testily, "it is about identifying the card. When the retailer sees Shakespeare, it triggers the correct procedures. Remember, retailers may be foreign or illiterate, but they can all be trained to recognize Shakespeare."

I did not pursue any of the hares which, at this, had leapt from cover. I merely said: "All right, how did you arrive at Shakespeare?"

"Well," said Jim, "we'd put Beethoven on our Euro-cheque card, and he went down very well. For example, he was not in any way political. So we thought: who is the domestic equivalent?"

"To what base uses we may return, Horatio!" I said. "I mean, Jim."

But I rang off cordially. After all, when you get right down to it, if imperious Caesar, dead and turn'd to clay, might stop a hole to keep the wind away, so what?

Provided it triggers the correct procedures in Tesco's.

Stands Cricklewood Where It Did?

This morning, *mutatis mutandis*, I might well have risen betimes, strolled out of my front gate, and – slicing with my trusty clasp-knife a stout blackthorn switch the better to negotiate my passage through Cricklewood's tangled undergrowth – picked my way daintily across the gently steaming midden of Cow House Farm, bound for the chimney-pot manufactory a mere country mile away, atop Child's Hill.

I should not, in all probability, have run into many people. The old gateman of Cricklewood House – at the bottom of my lane, beside the village pond – would doubtless have tugged his forelock as I passed, but dared to offer nothing more personal than his regular animadversion upon the fox-droppings scarring his gravel; the herdsman whittling in the Cow House Farm hedge might have had an interesting intelligence to impart anent the eccentric behaviour of his charges, adding a rider to the effect that it might do none of us any harm to lay off chops for a while; the buxom chatelaine of the Castle Tea Gardens might have leaned, dimpling, through her leaded lights, to murmur that there was nothing could set up a gentleman of a morning like a nice toasted scone; but I should be fortunate indeed to meet any others along the way, before heaving to at the premises of my old friend Jas Merry-weather, supplier of chimneys to the carriage trade, for one of our regular chats upon such burning issues of the day as the threat to family life of the Zoetrope or whether anyone in his right mind believed that the new Conservative Party's Tamworth Manifesto would enable it to break the traditional mould of British politics.

Oh yes, and I might also have bumped, as I meandered, into a stranger peering through a theodolite. Had I done so, I should have doffed my stovepipe hat, saying: "Good morning, sir, do I take it that a survey is under way? I trust it is not in consequence of this new Municipal Reform Act! You may tell your masters that any attempt to levy the proposed annual groat upon my humble cot will be met with the sternest resistance. Melbourne, Melbourne, Melbourne, out, out, out!"

He would have smiled a demurring smile, and extended his hand. "George Cruchley, sir," he would have said, "a humble cartographer and your yet humbler servant, engaged merely upon his map of Cricklewood."

"Pshaw!" I should have snorted. "We are nought but a bucolic speck of fourteen dwellings. Who are we to merit bespoke cartography?"

"A speck today, perhaps," he might have replied, "but it will not always be 1835. One day, who knows, the very knoll upon which we are standing may be graced by not merely Adrian's Unisex Hair Salon, but also Roxy Videos, Kutprice Kars, and the Hing Yip Takeaway."

How uncannily accurate he would have been!

So then, shall I recommend to the rest of you the sumptuous new book which lies open before me in this year of ungrace 1990, and which contains not only Cruchley's *New Plan*, but umpteen more magnificent old maps, spanning London, change by change, from one Elizabeth to the other? I'm not sure I ought. True, *The History of London in Maps*, by Felix Barker and Peter Jackson, will give contemporary metropolitans far more than merely 1p change from twenty quid, but will they be able to handle that gift any less mournfully than I? Will they, like me, hurtle first to the index to check for entry what was once, literally, their neck of the woods, only to reflect upon how utterly, between then and now, the woods got it in that very neck?

Ah, Cricklewood! There on page 98 you lie, forever panting and forever young, committed to ink in the year my great-grandfather was born; which, put that way, seems not so long ago. A baker's dozen of cottages, and the manor house, and a windmill on Shoot-Up Hill from which the miller could look across to Wilsdon Green when it was nothing but that; and to Hendon, when the site of ten thousand subsequent semis bore only Clatterhouse Farm; and to the Green Hill far away, when it was not yet Golder's, but simply what you climbed to get to the Hare and Hounds.

On a Wing and a Prayer

W e were just leaving Westley Waterless when it happened. We were just leaving Westley Waterless for the third time in an hour. But, lest a picture may have come into your mind of a man and a woman unable to get Westley Waterless out of their system, tearing themselves away from it only to hear it calling them back, it should quickly be said that what we were in fact attempting to do was get our system out of Westley Waterless.

The system had been carefully worked out, last Sunday afternoon, in a little orchard in the mid-Suffolk village of Stansfield, which is six miles from Westley Waterless as the crow flies, or 27 if the crow's wife is using the *Collins Road Atlas*. Let us, however, not rush to blame either the crow's wife or the *Collins Road Atlas*, partly because those who have tried this will know that it does not get them anywhere, but also because the Suffolk signposts have their own ideas about where anything is, and these only occasionally correspond with *Collins*'s opinion.

It may, of course, be that mid-Suffolk's mid-folk belong to the Ridleyite Tendency, and creep out at night to turn their signposts round to confuse Waffenbundesbank paratroops landing in Stansfield with a view to striking at the soft underbelly of Westley Waterless. Indeed, the hereinabove-mentioned system had not a little to do with such thoughts: Sunday was not only a hot afternoon, it was the fiftieth anniversary of another hot afternoon, and, lying on one's back in an East Anglian orchard, you did not have to be a former secretary for trade and industry to imagine the cerulean welkin embroidered, once again, with vapour trails. In such a mood, and in, moreover, an open tourer, what more apt a homeward system than via the meandering network of unchanged Suffolk back roads which thread redly across the *Collins* pages like the veins on a drunkard's conk?

So that is why we were here, nostalgically belting between the high hedgerows, when it happened. It, too, was belting between the high hedgerows, but it was belting transversely, from one hedgerow to another. A susceptible cove, your Johnny synapse, especially if its brain has been thinking about the Last Lot: in the nanosecond before the thing struck, I could have sworn it was an Me109. Then it hit the offside wing and somersaulted over our heads, and I saw, after I had braked and looked back, that it was a pheasant. I got out, slowly, with that grisly admixture of chagrin and dread one cannot but feel at the hurt of a fellow creature, but it was all right, there wasn't a mark on her, the no-claims bonus was safe. The bird, however, was stone dead.

I know little of the countryside, and less of its juridical arcana. While I know that you cannot kill pheasants in July, I do not know what happens to those who do. Nor do I know if different laws obtain regarding pheasants wild and raised; did this corpse belong to a bloke who had lovingly hand-reared it so that he could lovingly plug it next October, and if so, might I not owe him something? The road was deserted, which was one answer to all such questions. I opened the boot; I put the pheasant in. After all, just to leave it there would have made its death meaningless; as links in the food chain went, it was one of the plumper.

"I'm not pulling its stuff off," said my wife. "Or out."

"Just read the map," I said. "We don't wish to hang around Westley Waterless, now."

"We never did," said my wife, "but that didn't stop us."

We were, however, luckier this time. We found the way to Stump Cross, which is where you halt in order to have a row about whether to take the B184 or the M11. And, after a bit, to say hang on, what's that peculiar noise in the boot?

That little I know about the countryside does not embrace the habitat of pheasants. Is Essex all right for Suffolk ones? Not that I could have done anything about it if it wasn't; when I opened the lid, the corpse shot by me like a clay pigeon. Who knows, maybe it will find its way back to Westley Waterless? If, that is, it has the sense to ignore the signposts.

AUGUST

Sick Leave

While I yield to no one in my admiration either for medical science or for the industries which convert its unflagging research into tubes, phials, tins, jars, boxes and bubble-packs, there is no question but that their insistence on constant breakthroughs makes the prospect of each succeeding holiday exponentially glummer. Between your last trip and your next, they will invariably have come up with something new, and you will not only have to take it with you, you will have to confront the prospect of the suffering which will require you to unscrew it.

Once upon a time, and not so long ago at that, the travelling Briton was quite prepared to enter Abroad with nothing more prophylactic than a stout walking-stick and a red-spotted bandanna. It was all there was. Finding himself, say, in a noxious spot where the natives were dropping like flies, not to say because of them, the Briton would use the stick both to fend off anybody who might be falling towards him and to negotiate his passage over those who had already fallen, while holding the bandanna over his face to filter whatever it was that was felling them.

43

Alternatively, were he to sustain a fracture, it would be the matter of a moment to snap the stick into splints and convert the bandanna into a sling, or, in the event of a gash from tusk or kris, a tourniquet. He would then press on regardless, while things healed. The better sticks were hollow and contained whisky, but this was his only medicinal concession, reserved for that occasional moment when he contracted something from, say, a dodgy Ganges oyster or a suppurating Baluchi he might have inadvertently rubbed up against in the camel-queue, and had to go and lie down until the fever broke.

He did not let this spoil his holiday; even more important, he did not let its possibility spoil his anticipation of his holiday. Since there was nothing he could do about anything, there was no point worrying. That he might catch malaria while pottering the alien bogs did not cross his mind. Until, that is, word got out about quinine. He then began to fret. He felt he ought to take precautions. He bought a bottle.

I have just got back from the pharmacist. I have 19 packets. I have piriton, and anti-histamine, and sodium hypochlorite, and lomotil, and codeine, and flagyl, and pseudoephedrine, and chlorimazole, and chloramphenicol, and dextropropoxyphene, and benzocaine, and achromycin, and diethyl toluamide, and some of them you swallow, and some you smear on, and some you spray, and some you inhale, and I am only going to France. The last time I went, I had a mere 17 packets, but today the pharmacist said that there was a lot of something or other about and there were these new things on the market, so I bought them. He also enquired whether I had considered taking a plasma pack, since you couldn't trust foreign blood transfusions these days, and I thought, oh good, something new to worry about, I wonder if he's got any off-the-peg artificial hips, I bet French orthopaedics is a bit iffy, but I was up to thirty quid already.

All very sad. I am not a hypochondriac, and for the rest of the year I wait for something to go wrong before researching a cure, but here I am, forced to contemplate the thousand natural shocks that flesh is heir to, and, even worse, gloomily wondering if there's a 1001st I may have missed, suppose I got beriberi, suppose a goitre came up, or a wen, suppose I woke up deaf, would it be smart to get something for it now, rather than face some ghastly Gallic quack in a wine-stained goatee advancing upon me with a fistful of mildewed suppositories?

But at which point to stop? I ask only because of a handy tip from Moyra Bremner which I have just spotted in the *Daily Telegraph*: "If a sea-urchin spine becomes embedded in your skin while bathing, bandage a paw-paw or pineapple over it. The fruit's enzymes open up the skin, making removal easy."

Pity I didn't notice it earlier. The greengrocer's is bang next door to the chemist's.

A Star is Born

I may enrol in RADA when I get home. Nothing major, you understand, none of that speaking from the diaphragm stuff, or how to get the audience on your side when poking your eyes out. Nor is milking maximum yuks from hobbling through french windows with my trousers down my ambition.

What I am after is a crash course in thespian trimmings. I need a convincing yawn, an eyecatching stretch, a fetching smirk, an authentic loll. What might be called interesting sitting. I do not need the walk. I have the walk. Admittedly, it owes not a little to John Wayne, but it is none the worse for that, and, after all, someone had to pick up the fallen torch. Yesterday, I did his slow turn. Pinched it straight out of *The Searchers*. How could I not? I was framed in an archway, with the sun behind me. I kinked a hip, dropped a shoulder, turned, and ambled into the sunlight. It will be on your screens any day now. Try to catch it, if you live in Düsseldorf.

The director was an extremely nice chap. As a humble extra, I don't often meet my directors, but this one gave me his card. No fee, mind, but these are early days, and it was, after all, a pretty informal commission. Shall I get out of the way, I said (in French: this was an international co-production), and he said, non, non, non – indeed, would I mind walking through the archway, slowly, if this did not derange me? I am not deranged at all, I replied, and I did the thing with the hip and the shoulder, and it was a winner. You could tell that, because he made an O with his thumb and forefinger. No retakes. As I said, when it comes to the walk, I am a natural.

The sit is immeasurably trickier. I was in three major movies yesterday – two Japanese, one American – and I had to stay in my chair, at the café table, in the corner of the Cathedral Square in Vence. It is an extremely picturesque corner of the old town, which is why it is extremely pictured. You cannot sit there for two minutes without a tourist pottering through with his camcorder on his shoulder, often jabbering excitedly into its integral mike.

When I am down here, as I am this week, I am in the square most mornings; same café, same table. I arrive around 11am to get the papers, and a *grand express*, and a slug of something to scour the pipes. Now it just so happens that in order to get the best shot of the square, you have to include me in it. In the old days of snapshotting and silent ciné, this was a role so minor as to be irrelevant; indeed, dispensable. Photo of medieval square, bloke reading *Times* in corner, you either keep him in for the human touch or you crop him out. Similarly, with the old 8mm, if the bloke suddenly embarked upon some mood-reducing activity, such as picking his nose or slashing at a wasp with the Business section, you could, when you got back to Yokohama, edit him out.

But the camcorder has changed all that. Editing video-tape is an exceedingly difficult business. Monkey see, monkey shoot, monkey more or less stuck with result. Suddenly, a new incumbency is placed upon the uninvited actor. He can make or break this movie. When the director is back home, about to première *Herr Ingenieur Müller Fahrt Nach Frankreich* to a rapt neighbourhood audience, he may not want their attention distracted. He may not want his fascinating commentary on Romanesque façades interrupted by a query from the floor regarding the dingbat in the straw hat who has knocked his calvados into his trousers and begun shouting at God.

Look how I upset the first Jap yesterday. As his lens panned through me, I raised my glass in cheery salutation. He stepped back from his tripod and glared furiously. Had he been remaking *The Bridge on the River Kwai*, one felt, he would have had me in the tin outhouse in less time than it takes to tell. In consequence, I sat stone-faced for his compatriot. For the cheery American, however, I raised my sombrero. He will be able to tell the folks back home that I am a local character. Cézanne's illegitimate grandson, perhaps. His local Rotary will be knocked out.

Which is why I need RADA, if I am to make something of myself. A Donald Sinden eyebrow, an Antony Sher tic, a Derek Jacobi pout, can take you right to the top in this business.

Plum Centre

I have always been an iron. It enabled me to become a millionaire several times over. It made me something in the City, and far beyond: as an iron, I have been able not merely to knock them in the Old Kent Road, but also to control Fleet Street and bend Whitehall to my whim. I have had only to set foot in The Strand to have my adversaries cry "Goodbye, Piccadilly!" and "Farewell, Leicester Square!" and head, keening, for Carey Street.

Because the iron has not been content simply to flatten all before it, it has seen to it that in its steamrollering wake, houses, modest and elegant, have risen, and hotels, seedy and swish, and all of them nice little earners. It has not only privatised water and electricity and watched both flourish beneath its iron management, but even, *mirabile dictu*, run the railways at an enormous profit. That its career has not been entirely unchequered has mattered nary a whit: though on occasion it has gone straight to jail, that infallible good fortune which favours the brave has ensured that it has gone straight out again, whereafter it has simply gone straight. And straight, moreover, to the top.

What persuaded me, all those years ago, to be an iron? I could, after all, have been a top hat, a roadster, a dog, a boot; all of them – when it comes to the feral cut and thrust of the property business – with more self-evident metaphorical clout. For what is the top hat but smoothly inherited wealth exponentially increasing beneath the magic wheels of the perpetual Grosvenor Estates machine? And what is the roadster but a flash huckster in a tattersall waistcoat snapping up pensioners' cottages by virtue (if that is the word) of imminent-motorway stories, and what the dog and boot (when it is not an iffy East End pub) but the twin henchmen of Rachmanism?

No. I was a moral kid, at 12, and shunned the taint of these. When, that 1950 Christmas, my old man came across with the Monopoly set, I plumped for the iron, and my modesty has never since gone unrewarded. The iron carried no metaphorical baggage, save the resonances of hard work, humility, and straightforwardness. Its only maxim was that it struck while it was hot, and I have thought of that as no bad watchword for the fickle world of speculation on many occasions since, as the last of my fellow players was finally compelled to tip his sole remaining hovel into the cardboard compartment provided, cash in his nugatory chips, and wander, broke and broken, into the rising dawn.

Where, at 2am this morning, and for the first time in my life, I find myself; and in France of all places, a spot already so deeply suspicious of Britain's commercial ineptitude as to need no such sops to its bigotry as the knocking-out, from our village Monopoly contest, of the debonair Londoner with the street-smart chuckle and the big cigar, both of which burned out in concert with his fortunes as the evening deepened. I have been cleaned out, and humiliated; and you know why?

Because I have been a plum. Bad enough in English, it is worse in French. I have been a *prune*. They do not have irons, here. They do not even have top hats and dogs and roadsters and boots. In Provence, they play Monopoly with little plastic fruit. How do you assess the fiduciary acumen of a raspberry, a banana or a fig? I was allotted the *prune*. And it got clobbered: it rarely went past *départ* to collect its 20,000 francs, it always went to *prison*, and it never got out without a fine. Every time it hit *chance* or *caisse de communauté*, it copped a penalty. *Erreur de la banque en votre faveur?* Fat chance! *La vente de votre stock vous rap-*

porte F5,000? Ha! It owned nothing, except, briefly, the Rue de la Paix, where nobody landed, not even the coconut, who had never played before. Whenever it appeared, creeping round a corner, the other fruit cried, *"Elle vient, la prune!"*, knowing it would be all right, the *prune* would land on them.

It invariably did. But as I, the game's first casualty, slumped from Le Café du Midi to alien sniggers, I could not forbear from crying, *"Normalement, je suis un fer à repasser"*. They did not even look up.

The Story of Eau

You'd get a lot more out of this if it were being written by a Frenchman. Or a German. Any European, actually, save an Englishman. You would get a lot more out because they would put a lot more in. You wouldn't know they had put a lot more in, mind, until you'd finished it; when you would think for a bit, and say to yourself, "Something tells me there's more in this than meets the eye. I think this foreign johnny's being a bit allegorical".

You would not be wrong. Turn this snippet's grist over to Albert Camus or Günther Grass, and face value would be out of the window before you could say magic realism. Not a word would be typed without its cryptic *Doppelgänger* lurking in its shadow, waiting to hijack its ostensible meaning. You would have to conclude this piece wasn't about doomed bougainvillaea and cleaning your teeth in Perrier, but about the Occupation, or the sacrament, or almost any-

50

thing except the fact that the mayor is going to cut the water off unless the village stops illicit sprinkling.

You are, however, safe with me. A simple English journey-hack, I have scant truck with symbolic gubbins. Though I catch, from their furtive eyes and their eavesdropped polyglot mutters, my fellow-villagers' sense that *une comédie humaine* is being played out here, that a *Zeitgeist* is raising its Janus head, that we are all standing *nel mezzo del cammin di nostra vita*. What I say is that it is a water shortage, no more, no less, and that is why everyone is behaving as they are.

The municipal two-stroke came by again this morning, grinding up the hill beside our cottage, and bleating through its ambilingual megaphone: *"Use water only for personal hygiene! No watering of the garden! No washing of the cars! No unnecessary laundering! All infringements will have the gravity of section 18 of the mayoral decree!"* Then in French. Never in German or Dutch or Italian, though this Provençal commune sports as multinational a summer tenancy as you could shake a quill at, if, as I say, you were some alien laureate bent on banging out one of those microcosmic jobs with which the Penguin Classics teem.

It makes the Englishman deeply unsettled to be thus uniquely selected. Takes you back to those morning assemblies where a rage-quivering beak committed himself to getting to the bottom of the desecration of the bicycle shed, and five hundred innocents felt, willy-nilly, the blood rise up their necks. When I drove into the village this morning for a couple of bottles of Evian for the geraniums, I could feel a hundred eyes staring at the car. Fortunately, it was still fly-encrusted from the autoroute. My shorts had seen cleaner days, too. This is a time when village mothers send their kids to school in dirty underwear, in case they get knocked down.

The Provençal drought is now three months old. Brown is almost everywhere. Where it is not, sly men peer over fences, cock ears, sniff. Why has that hibiscus bloomed overnight, why is that lawn suddenly viridescent? Villagers are

51

reporting one another to the authorities, the curé has preached a sermon on the proximity of self-denial to godliness, the farmers have circulated a petition about pool-owners and their civic duties, and the Vichy café and the Gaullist café dream of catching one another covertly sluicing down the pavement.

Ostentation is manufacturing suspicion. Anyone taking a bar of soap into the village fountain is immediately suspected of nocturnal hosing. People walking matted dogs are suffering close scrutiny of their pot plants. Sanctimoniously unshaven men could find themselves having their heads publicly cropped when this is all over, on the grounds it was all a front to disguise what was going on in their hanging baskets. The nights are worst: sprinklers sound like Lewis guns, and neighbouring lights snap on, and it is no good claiming, after you have run round turning off the taps, that the noise was the cicadas up to their old tricks, because the moonlight sets the drops on your oleander winking, and it is useless trying to pass it off as cricket-widdle.

Sign Language

D'ye ken Jean-Paul? With his *cotier gris*?
'Twas the sound of his horn called me from my bed . . .

Yesterday, and yesterday, and yesterday, to the first syllable of recorded holiday, Jean-Paul has crept in his petty pace from day to day, full of sound and fury, signifying nothing except that the road bends outside our Provençal door. For the bend is, as literally as a cliché ever gets, a red rag to a bull: when Jean-Paul spots a bend, he puts his head down, boots his *cotier gris* out of its petty pace, flares his electric nostrils so that the bellow echoes from hill to hill, and charges at it. As with all red rags, there is nothing on the other side, but, as with all bulls, Jean-Paul hasn't yet twigged this.

Nor is he alone; no Ferdinand he. At the break of day, if you will allow one more poetical conflation, a lowing herd winds slowly past my *lit*. They are all *cotiers gris*, those grey 2CV tricycle-vans whose engines are based on the maracas principle: you put a lot of old bolts in a cocoa tin and, provided you shake them noisily enough, the wheels go round. I do not know how this works, I know only that it enables me to ken Jean-Paul when he's far, far away; so that when the break of day brings him to the bottom of the hill, I wake up, and when, five minutes later, he blows his horn at the bend, I am called from my bed, because there is no point lying there trying to kid yourself that there will not be another one along in a minute.

Nothing more separates our cultures than our hooter strategies. The French honk to signal what might happen in the future, the British to signal what has happened in the past. The English hoot is a mechanical oath, expressing an opinion as to what another driver should not have done, the French hoot is a monitory cry, warning a driver of what he might be about to do. That is why they call them *avertisseurs*.

Since a French driver might be about to do anything at any time, the hooter is in constant use. Only this morning, I noticed that le Kwikfit at Nice not only replaces exhausts, it replaces *avertisseurs*, too. Has any English hooter ever worn out?

It was not all I noticed. Driving up the hill from Nice to Vence, I passed a road-sign. It said *Ni Vitesse, Ni Bruit*. I did not pass it far. I pulled over. I strolled back, as one ravished by the view, a Midiphile looking now towards the sun-winking Med, now towards the soft ochre tumble of St Paul; someone to whom you would have to get very close in order to spot what was going on in the corners of those ostensibly beguiled eyes. The sign was fastened to its post by two nuts. The corners of the eyes grew yet beadier.

I eased a spanner from the car's tool-kit. One nut came off as if buttered. The sign hinged downward from the other, with a slight squeak. I quickly put my shoulder beneath it, to level it to inconspicuousness, at which moment a car came up the hill; leaving me no option but to turn my back, lower one arm, and offer the driver the sheepish smirk of the enuretic.

He disappeared over the crest. The second nut yielded. I walked back to my car like a man carrying a road-sign. An hour later, outside my house, a hitherto unofficial tree now made it illegal to speed or honk.

"What have you been doing?" said my wife.

"Oh, this and that," I said. The less she knew, the better. With both of us on Devil's Island, our kids would run amok. (Though, if apprehended, I plan to approach the French bench with that arcane Cricklewood law, *lex itinerandum*, i.e., I have not broken the law, I have merely moved it somewhere else.) "What about you?"

"I've been reading Anthony West's biography of Wells," she replied. "Did you know that Wells built a house for his mistress Odette Keun just along our road, near Grasse? West says he used to infuriate the locals by driving everywhere with his thumb on the hooter. I wonder if that's where the French learnt it?"

I looked at the sky. I sipped my gin. They can be a curious shape, the things to come.

Japanese Sandmen

I have returned to Cricklewood to find that our local futon centre has closed down. I realize that, in the great roster of homecoming trauma, this ranks somewhere below Odysseus's dog dropping dead or Scarlett's discovery that Tara is going to need a bob or two spent on fixtures and fittings, but nevertheless it has come as a considerable shock.

Not because the closure spells, I suspect, the end of some sort of era, nor even because, in the nine years during which I have driven past it every day, the futon centre has become a much-loved feature of the landscape, but because I never once, in all those thousands of days, stopped and walked into it to find out what a futon was. I shall never walk into it now, and I shall never know.

Mind you – were I to be utterly honest – I cannot be certain that I should ever have plucked up the courage to do it. The time for asking what a futon was passed some years ago. You have to be quick off the blocks with fad-enquiries, if you do not wish to sound like a high court judge looking up from his jotting quill to enquire of the clerk what a hula-hoop is when it's at home. Even in the matter of bedding: I asked what a duvet was as soon as I heard the word, and to this day I get cold shudders when I think of the ridicule a week's delay would have invited. As for futons, one morning they did not exist, and the next morning, it seemed, everyone except me was banging on about them with remarkable authority. Since I tended to sidle away from these conversations in case I was exposed, I never did discover what they were, and soon everyone had stopped discussing them and gone on to cellphones and gravad lax, and it was too late.

Now, lest you begin to think me so untouchable a nerd that the authority of this entire opus is undermined, I should quickly say that I know *roughly* what a futon is. I can drag the new *OED* from its shelf as deftly as the next Waterstone browser, and I can read that a futon is a Japanese bed-quilt. This of course tells me nothing at all. Nor do the two quotations the OUP has dug up to endorse this definition, although they go back an astonishing long way for a fad, to 1876 and 1886 respectively. The first, taken from the *Transactions of the Asiatic Society of Japan*, cites: "Those who are tired of tinned meats and live futons", and the second, attributed to one E.S. Morse, says: "The futons, or comforters, are hung over the balcony rail to air."

I quote these arcana in their entirety. It is obvious that both Mr Morse and the Hon Sec of the ASJ were devout Nipponophiles attempting to curry face by showing that the round-eyes, too, are dab hands when it comes to banging out impenetrable *haikus*. I have little doubt that the latter gobbet does not mean what it superficially appears to say at all, and probably refers to the insolence of princes or something, and as for the former, it is a yen to a threepenny-bit that you could sit 50 structuralists in front of their decoders till Doomsday and they would never even come close.

No, when I say I do not know what futons are, I do not mean I do not know they are some kind of Japanese bedding (I have, after all, caught glimpses of them in the now-whitewashed window these nine years past); I mean that I do not know what is special about them. I have no idea what futonness comprises. What is the essence of its difference from a posture-sprung Slumberland, a chaise-longue, a hammock? Why, on that bright confident morning a decade ago, did everyone who was anyone, from Campden Hill to Tuscany, suddenly and simultaneously become excited by them?

I suppose it sprang from our peculiar conviction that Orientals have cracked the secret of relaxation. They do go on about it rather a lot. Five minutes in the lotus position, a couple of mantras, a quick tot of ginseng, a pull or two on the old Zen bow, and then into the futon for a good night's kip and next morning you're fresh as a daisy.

That may be *onto* the futon, of course, or under it, or even between them, if they come in twos; I wouldn't know, and I very much doubt, now, that I ever shall.

SEPTEMBER

Uneasy Lies the Head

If for nothing else, today's *feuilleton* will be remarkable for recording the smallest thing ever to go wrong with a house in its owners' absence. Indeed, so confident am I of this claim that if any reader writes to me with a smaller, he will receive, by return of post, a magnum of the finest Toblerone.

I spent the Bank Holiday weekend in Edinburgh, where it turned out not to be a Bank Holiday at all; so that I came home feeling oddly deprived. It was not for some time that I discovered the yet odder depths to which deprivation may plummet.

It was four hours, to be precise; which is precisely what I can be. I know that my key turned in the lock at 3pm, because I heard the cuckoo clock in the kitchen observe this; just as I know that it was 7pm when I discovered what I discovered, because I was in the kitchen itself at the time, slicing the lemon for the yard-arm gin, and when the clock cuckooed, I looked up.

Owners of clocks of the order *cuculidae* will not need an explanation for this, but the rest of you might be thunder-

61

struck to learn that that is what you do if you are in a room with one at any time after five o'clock. Up until five o'clock, the number of cries registers in the head, but after that time you have no idea how many it is, and you have to look up at the clock to see what hour it is.

I looked up just in time to see the little door shutting. And, in the nanosecond before it did, to note that what it was shutting on was not the cuckoo.

I walked across to the clock, prised open the door with my forefinger, and peered into the cuckoo's premises. It was not there. It had flown its tiny coop. To make doubly sure, I forefingered the minute-hand around to eight o'clock: the door burst open, the voice cried eight times, but what leapt out on each of these eight occasions was nought but a wobbling spring. The cuckoo was not on the end of it.

Where had it gone? And why? Had it, perhaps, in ecstasy at finding it had the house to itself, hurtled so joyously from its cavity that it had detached itself from its tiny umbilicus? Or heard, maybe, the rumour of a sparrow-clock somewhere, and gone off to lay an egg in it?

Unlikely. It is, in truth, only half a cuckoo. It is little more than a head on a spring. I cannot speak for more expensive clocks, it may well be that the Swiss houses of parliament sport a giant example which hourly lurches from its penthouse atop Big Bird intact in every particular, but mine, sadly, does not have the wherewithal to parturiate. It does not even have legs. It could not have gone far. I searched the kitchen floor. Nothing.

Had a clockwork cat got in?

I wondered if the head might have fallen off not forwards at all, but backwards. It could be lying on the floor of the works, struggling ventriloquially every time the spring sprang out. It dawned upon me that Wordsworth must have suffered similar horological shock; nothing else could explain so awful a line as "O Cuckoo! Shall I call thee bird, or but a wandering voice?" It is exactly what the old fool would have cried upon walking into Dove Cottage to find himself confronted with a headless chime.

I took the clock from the wall, and removed the back, appropriately enough, with my Swiss Army knife. Exactly, I'm sure, what the Swiss Army would have done in the circumstances. The head was not inside.

Three days have now passed, and some 50 phone calls. Can you believe that there is not a spare cuckoo head to be found anywhere in these islands? I tried this morning to fashion one from Plasticine, with a little matchstick beak, but it was too heavy, it lumbered out on the first cry, hung dangling over the clockface, and refused to go back until manhandled.

I do now know what to do. I may have to junk the clock. The kitchen is below my bedroom, I hear the cry in the small hours, and I would swear a derisory note has crept into it. They do change their tune, you know.

Going for the Runs

In a world racked with imponderables, I find myself today preoccupied with one question only: have I been a good son to Jeffrey Archer? Was he proud of me? Did I say the right things? Did I use the right fork? Were my shoes clean? Did I drink too much?

These things are important.

Dad rang me on Friday night. I was in the bath, but I took the call because who knew when Dad might have another window? Five minutes later, and he might be launched upon a new novel, flying to Tokyo to open a hot-dog stand, enthusing 10,000 Godalming Tories with visions of broad sunlit uplands, or parachuting into Baghdad with a personal message from the prime minister on the end of his Dunhill truncheon.

Saturday, however, was free. Jeffrey's cheery bark blew the soap from my ear to explain that young Jamie Archer would not be accompanying his father to the NatWest final, and I had therefore no other option than to be outside the Grace Gate at 10.14 upon the morrow morn, as substitute.

He was nearly nine seconds late. "Traffic," he explained. I got in his car, and we hurtled round to the North Gate.

"You can't park inside today," I said. "Anyway, it's shut."

Dad's bumper nudged the ironwork. Two stewards sprang. You know MCC stewards. On their days off, they chase Rottweilers.

"Good morning!" cried Dad.

"Oh, it's Mr Archer!" Scour *Wisden*, and tell me when an MCC steward last beamed.

He shook their hands. He knew their names. The gates opened.

"These things are important," said Dad.

He shook a lot more hands on the scuttle to our box. So did I. Dad would say to me, "I don't think you know . . .", thumbs would enwrap, and I now know four policemen, two ground staff, an ex-England rugger captain, his three friends, and half a dozen other valuable contacts, including, as I recall, the shrewdest baronet in all England. This more than made up for missing the fall of the first wicket, and – since DeFreitas was singularly on song – the second, too, because as we arrived in the box, it was of course essential to establish whether I knew Lord and Lady Alexander, the Chancellor of the Exchequer, Freddie Trueman, and some two dozen other delightful companions, a process which allowed Fordham of Northants to avoid the embarrassment of having me see him stick his pad where his bat should have been.

Everyone then ran inside to watch it on the television replay, leaving Dad at something of a loose end. Fortunately, however, Cecil Parkinson was in the next box. I discovered this when I heard my name shouted, and there was Dad, magically teleported to the other side of the railing, whence he excitedly beckoned me, because he didn't know whether I knew either Cecil or Ann, or, as soon as I did, Sirs Leon Brittan or Christopher Tugendhat, either.

That I now do seems a small price to pay for having my back to both Larkins and Bailey while they were severally snicking stuff into the keeper's haberdashery. Nor should I not have been delighted to cement my new friendship had time, sadly, not been of the essence. Dad flew, and I followed.

"Glad Cecil's stopped putting grease on his hair," puffed Dad, as we sprinted the encircling corridor, "these things are important." And, breaking stride only to ascertain whether I knew Julian Holloway, two somewhat flustered WPCs, and the smartest banker in all Europe, he suddenly flung himself into another box, and I fell, gasping, after him.

An astonishing spot. Hardly had I established lifelong friendships with Sir Leonard Hutton, P.B.H. May, Mike Gatting, Brian Johnston, Doug Insole and a host of their chums and relatives, than I felt Dad dragging my sleeve towards R.E.S. Wyatt to find out whether I knew England's oldest surviving cricket captain. As I bent to shake his hand, Lamb became DeFreitas's fifth scalp.

An inswinger, I discovered from Sunday's paper. Not that these things are important.

A Brush with the Council

This morning, I shall have to proceed with particular caution. For mine is a highly sophisticated readership, and I say this not simply to butter it up; although, admittedly, it can't hurt to butter it up a bit, given where its sophistication might very well lead it, should my particular caution not come up to snuff. That is because my readership is so sophisticated that it knows what the Delphic audience did to Aesop when they took against the moralistic tone of his witterings. They chucked him over a cliff.

Ever since then, those with a fable to offload have had to proceed with particular caution. Doing it somewhere cliffless is a good start, but the best thing is a good finish, and a good finish means: no moral. Nothing in italics at the end, pointing the audience towards the homiletic pith. That is what got up their noses at Delphi. Nobody likes being told what they are supposed to have understood.

So what follows is just a fable. Make of it what you will. You will get no help from me. It is called *The Fox and the Cellphone*.

There was once a man who found himself, on a sunny September morning, standing on Kentish Town Railway Station. Kentish Town Railway Station is part of Network SouthEast, which is what the man himself wanted to be, only nothing came to net him and work him towards Cricklewood. He had been standing on the platform, alone, for 20 minutes, and this conjunction of time and solitude bothered him not a little, because he had seen *North by North-West*, and – being a susceptible sort of a man – he kept squinting up at the sky, just in case a biplane had any plans to dive on to him. You never knew, it was a funny old world, and just because you were going south by SouthEast, it didn't mean you shouldn't remain on your guard.

At the 21st minute, the man became aware of something approaching, down the track. It was not a train, it was not even a biplane coming in at zero altitude, it was a fox. It was trotting alongside the live rail, with a rat in its mouth. When it saw the man, it stopped. The man knew there was no point in asking it whether it had seen anything of the 10.14, because foxes have got smarter since Aesop's day and they know that if they open their mouths to speak, their food will drop out, and they are not going to be caught that way twice.

Something, however, did speak. It said "bloody hell", and when the man turned, he saw that he had been joined by another man, thirty-ish, snappily suited, who must have just come up the stairs from the booking-office. "Look at that," he continued, "I think I'd better tell someone about that," and he ran down the stairs again. At the clatter, the fox turned, and began trotting back the way it had come.

The second man returned, flushed, clearly angry.

"They don't give a toss!" he cried. "They say they get foxes here all the time. I pointed out all the risks, but they don't give a toss."

"More than their job's worth, no doubt," said the man from Cricklewood, in jocular vein, for he did not wish to offend the stranger, who, despite the smart cut of his jib, might well be a homicidal crop-duster who had parked his biplane round the corner to divert suspicion.

"Not only could it cause a derailment," said the stranger, "it is a dangerous and verminous animal. We have," he added, "just moved in here. We've got small children! I'm phoning the council."

Whereupon he opened his briefcase, took out a portable telephone, and began punching buttons. That he knew the

67

council's number was not lost on the first man: here, clearly, was someone who got things done.

But not always. For, after a moment or two, the stranger swore and shook the phone. "Sodding battery's flat," he said. "Can you believe it?"

The man from Cricklewood might have replied, had the train, at that moment, not appeared, encouraging the distant fox to hop delicately off the track and disappear. He might also have wondered which of his two new companions was the more likely to survive in Kentish Town. But he would not, of course, have said anything, because the area was unfamiliar to him, and could well have a cliff somewhere.

Tunnel Vision

Cheated by last Friday's weather of the early-morning tennis-game which – such is my canniness in dietary negotiation – buys me the right to a lunchtime Scotch, I decided instead to do something I had not done since I had done it in short trousers, a scuff-shoed crocodile, and abject misery. I decided to go for a nice bracing swim in a public pool.

Accordingly, I turned up at Swiss Cottage, that site for eyesores taken full advantage of by Sir Basil Spence's famous leisure centure – an off-white blockhouse in the engaging post-Maginot style, encrusted with a job lot of neo-Aztec carvings generously donated, after a short, fierce struggle, by local ratepayers – bought a ticket to one of its three indoor swimming pools, and went inside.

It was like Proust sinking his canine into a moist macaroon, a lousy description, admittedly, of a public baths except insofar as with that first whiff of chlorine, that first glance at the trembling ripples of light which water makes on tiles, that first faint reverberation of the hollow echoes which bark only in swimming pools, I was back 40 years, in that wet shivering line of bony white homunculi, milk-teeth chattering and gooseflesh bubbling like tripe, waiting for some track-suited sadist to boot us into the deep end for the good of our souls.

When I returned from the changing cubicle, the pool was empty.

There was, however, one man looking at it. About 70, pear-shaped, with a belly of delicately veined white Ferrara marble, his hands behind his back, and a bald pink skull from which two small eyes were watching the water, very closely.

"See that!" he cried, suddenly, not looking up.

"What?" I said.

"That ripple thing, going up the pool!" I looked. A curious little wave, the full width of the pool, was running quickly up its length. "That'll be the 8.06," said the pear-shaped man.

"I'm sorry?"

"They built this right over the Bakerloo Line. When a tube pulls out of Swiss Cottage, you can see the vibration belting along the surface. It's all to do with . . ." he tailed off. "I'm not a scientist," he said.

"Are you going in?" I enquired.

"Oh, no," he said, looking at me for the first time. "I never go in here."

I walked to the springboard, wondering where it was that he did go in. When I came up gasping, numb from the follicles down, I found him yelling even more excitedly than before. "New wave's just passed you!" he shrieked. "Go on!"

I struck out desperately. I must be a natural subordinate.

"Too late!" cried the old man, highly delighted. "She'll be in St John's Wood before you've done a length."

It's a bizarre sensation, racing a tube-train down a swimming pool: here is the swimmer, naked man equipped only with his own feebleness, splashing across London in frantic pursuit of a cylinderful of suited office-staff reading the newspaper 50ft down. I fetched up against the shallow end, with a lifetime of dissipation knocking at my ribs.

"It beat me," I croaked.

"Course it did!" shouted the old bloke, "course it did! It always does. I never seen nobody beat it."

You don't ask a man whether he comes to a swimming pool at dawn every day just to watch fools racing ripples, mainly because you wouldn't know what to do with the answer if you had it. I dragged myself out and, as I did so, a wiry middle-aged woman in a thick woolly bathing-suit crept to the edge of the deep end, and slid in noiselessly.

"She used to be the Southern Counties Backstroke Champion," the audience confided as I towelled, "and even she can't beat it. It's accelerating as it leaves the station, see? It's prob'ly doing 20 miles a hour, time it gets up the deep end."

I dressed, and left. On the street, an icy wind cut across my soaking scalp, bringing a promise of early pneumonia and I hurried to my car; but not so quickly that I failed to catch sight of the opposition. At Swiss Cottage station mufflered men in a long line were filing into the booking hall, totally unaware that they were about to take on the former Southern Counties Backstroke Champion.

Least of the Few

When I look back, all these years on, to that fateful golden summer, it seems madness to have sent kids out in crates like that. But we went, because we had to.

Expert hands helped us struggle into the one-piece suit, and they zipped it up, and they helped us into the helmet and the boots, and after we had climbed into the tiny close-fitting seat, they adjusted the safety harness over our shoulders and closed the canopy above us, and the next thing we knew the wheels were lurching over the bumpy ground, and we were away, and there was no turning back.

I don't know if you remember the old Dunkley. Even by the standards of 1940, it was a pig of a machine. Heavy and slow, it squeaked, it rattled, it yawed, it shook, and no matter how experienced the hands on its controls, its lack of manoeuvrability was a constant threat. My mother was pretty good, but she never got it down the front steps without my head banging the side-struts, and 50 years on, I still can't look at a kerbstone without feeling a tweak in the coccyx. I do not know what push-chairs the Jerries had, but it's a safe bet they would have run rings round ours.

I make no apology for all this reminiscent gush. Last week-end, as the Spitfires thrummed above the Mall and men with arcane nicknames strolled nostalgic tarmacs and tugged at moustaches long past their ginger prime, I too set off upon a jubilee pilgrimage. I went to Chipperfield. Specifically, I went to The Boot.

I had not been to Chipperfield for 50 years. I do not know why, because it had always loomed large in the memory, and it lies a mere half-hour NW of Cricklewood, at the foot of the Chilterns; it may simply be that the significance of a visit was such that the time had to be momentous. Last weekend, however, could not have been more so, and I seized the day. I wished to wallow.

As much as anything else, I wished to verify memory. Two is, after all, an impressionable age, the stuff had been impressed, it was all there somewhere, I had retained a few disparate images, I wanted to know if a revisit would jog others, knit the snapshots into a flickering continuum, like those little booklets there used to be which, thumbed at the right speed, brought Wally Hammond's cover drive to life.

Astonishingly, that is precisely what happened. By some benevolent fortune, Chipperfield had not changed at all: the village green sprang to recollected life as in some pop-up book, and in the nanosecond before I actually saw The Two Brewers which dominates its further end, I knew exactly what it looked like, even though I had forgotten that it was there.

It was probably the first thing I had seen in the summer of 1940 when my father, always a man to hedge his bets, simultaneously joined the RAF and shipped my mother and me out of London on the offchance that his joining up was not going to be enough to change Hitler's mind.

I did not, however, drink at The Two Brewers last Saturday. As I looked at it, it suddenly came to me that our pub had been The Boot. The sign had materialized in my head. I asked where The Boot was, and I walked half a mile down the road, and it was. The last time I had gone down that road I had not walked, I had been pushed in the Dunkley. The Boot still had a garden, but I did not have to sit in it in the Dunkley, now, at 52, they let you drink inside.

"Pint of bitter," I said. "I haven't been here," I added, "for 50 years."

"Adnam's?" enquired the lad behind the bar.

"Fine," I said. "Yes, half a century. Doesn't appear to have changed."

"Would you like a menu?" said the lad.

"I'll have a gammon sandwich," I said. "Seems like yesterday, 1940."

"Wholemeal," said the lad, "or white?"

"White," I said. "Yes, it was a hot summer then, too, and . . ."

But he had gone, to relay my order. Kids today, what do they care? I did consider pointing out that I had spent my best years strapped in a bloody Dunkley for the likes of him, but I decided against it. He wouldn't have had the first idea of what I was talking about.

Max Minor

We had Max to stay for the weekend. He came on Thursday evening, and he left an hour ago, and what I am currently wondering is whether the experiences of this weekend will affect Max for the rest of his life.

Not that any of those experiences seemed momentous at the time. It was a normal weekend, a few meals, a few drinks, and, as you would expect from Max, if you knew him, a few laughs. Max is a gas. At dinner on Thursday, Max put his spoon in his ear, got a laugh, and never looked back. Did the spoon routine three days running. Got a laugh every time.

Whether it will be incorporated into his permanent reper-toire, time alone will tell. Tommy Cooper did the hat num-ber for 30 years. The spoon act doesn't bother me. Were you wondering what did bother me, the magic door would be a good place to start.

We were in the green bathroom at the time. Max took me aside after dinner and confided his pressing need, so I showed him to the green bathroom, and when he saw it he was knocked out. He had never seen a green bathroom before. His bathroom at home was blue, he said. He became so animated about the green bathroom, he could think of little else. He forgot why he was there. I reminded him. Max pointed out that the bathroom cabinet was green. He asked if he could open its door. I said it was a magic door, and it opened only when you did a wee-wee. You know the rest. The magic door opened a lot during the next four days.

Friday lunchtime there was nobody else about, so Max and I played with our food. We had a terrific time. Who would think you could build a passable elephant out of mashed potato? And once you've built it and it has a name, how can you possibly eat it? You eat ice-cream instead. Then, if you're two years old, it gives you an idea. You want to go to the Zoo. The person you're lunching with doesn't want to go to the Zoo, but if you turn your lip down, he chucks in the sponge. He would not if he were your father or mother, but your father and mother are in Paris, and you have not been slow to twig that an uncle is a pushover. If you do not want to wear your coat for the Zoo and your uncle tries to get you into your coat, after a bit your uncle says oh what the hell.

That is the difference between uncles and fathers. Fathers are inflexible because fathers have responsibilities. With fathers, you sit there until all the mashed potato is eaten; with fathers, you wear your coat when you go out, or you don't go out. Fathers tell themselves that ground rules have to be laid down early. Fathers are sticklers for the acorn-oak theory. Fathers are a pain in the nappy.

Fathers treat zoos as educational opportunities. If, however, you tell an uncle three times that a polar bear is a lion, an uncle says oh what the hell. Nor does an uncle know whether your parents demand-feed you Smarties. Or care. He wants you to have a good time. Fathers don't want you to have a good time. Fathers want you to have a clean face so that one day you can be a big cheese in corporate finance.

They want you to be healthy, wealthy and wise. Uncles, on the other hand, should you reappear at 9.30pm, dragging a teddy by its ear through the middle of *Jeeves and Wooster*, will chortle at your identification of Stephen Fry as Postman Pat, and let you stay up.

They also differ markedly from fathers on the question of literature. Fathers wish to instil respect for books as the precious life-blood of a master spirit. Uncles, should you begin pulling books from the shelves, will actually help you build them into a house, and if the one book big enough for a door happens to be *Hogarth's Complete Engravings*, an item only marginally improved by chocolate thumbprints, what the hell.

But, as I watched him toddle down the path just now, I felt a slight unease. Life's programming is a capricious enterprise: the odd rogue moment may wield disproportionate influence. If Kane hadn't had a sledge called Rosebud . . .

So this was written for Max. Just in case, one distant day, he wonders why he can't eat mashed potato. Never mind the curious business with the magic door.

OCTOBER

First Things First

I f there were a word to describe today's theme, I would be on the way to immortality. Your grandchildren could look the word up in encyclopaedias, where they would discover that I was the one who had discovered what they were looking up.

But have I? Can I be sure that what I have discovered has not been known all along? Is it simply that it has never had a word to describe it? That is the problem with hitting upon a concept, which is what my thing is, as opposed to an object: with an object, there is no dispute.

If you invent a steam engine, or a spinning jenny, or a water-closet, or any of the other things people are always looking up, there is no question but that you have invented it, because when you chug past, or weave something, or flush something else, people will cry: "Stone me! I have never seen anything like that before!" An invented object is indisputable proof of its own originality.

This is not the case with a concept. It could well have been thought of in a different place, at another time, by someone else; but since they could not come up with a word to describe it, nobody knew. Indeed, it is quite likely that after I have disclosed the concept I have discovered, letters will pour in from other claimants. Their grandchildren, even.

Perhaps the most galling element of all is that I came up with it in the bath. Or, rather, that Archimedes came up with his in the bath. Because if Archimedes had not come up with his in the bath, I should not have needed a word to describe my thing in order to ensure immortality. I could have got by on what I shouted. For every person who knows what Archimedes' theory was, there are 100 who do not know, but who know what he shouted when he discovered it. If you don't believe me, get a grandchild to look it up in the *Shorter Oxford*.

I would not myself have cried Eureka!, of course. Your grandchildren would have had to look up Blimey!, or some such. But it would have been no less immortal for that. Nor was the bath itself any less essential to the discovery of my theory than Archimedes' bath was to his. Indeed, mine has the edge, in that it is a two-bath theory: though it was discovered in Saturday afternoon's bath, it could not have been discovered without Saturday morning's.

Which was when I let myself out of the bath only to find that I could not do the same for the bathwater. The plug would not come out of its hole. It is supposed to do this when I turn a knurled knob on the wall above the bath, since the knob is attached to a clever linkage of levers and cogs hidden behind the tiling. The cleverest thing about this being the plumber who persuaded me 18 years ago that no modern bathroom should be without a mechanical plug. That mine now was, I discovered an hour later, having removed the bath panel to find that the linkage of levers was not as clever as I thought it was, otherwise it would not be lying under the bath in bits.

I see the end of this chapter approaching, and must cut a long story short, particularly since that is an analogue of the story itself. The long plug became short. The plumber I called out said, yes, well removing the tiling etcetera, we could well be looking at the wrong end of 400 quid here, and after the red mist had ebbed, I said is there no alternative, and he said what about a rubber one on a chain, can't go wrong there, I've got one in the van.

It was while I was lying in the second bath necessitated by crawling around under the first one, and idly twisting my new chain around my toe, that the theory suddenly came to me. Things get invented in the wrong order. If man had always had clever linkages, would the rubber plug not be seen as an extraordinary breakthrough?

Had television been invented first, would we not bless the genius who subsequently came up with the radio? Is a threepenny box of matches not the answer for all who mourn lost gold cigarette lighters, or the pencil not the wondrous boon that might have replaced the word-processor?

And might my theory not have made the world an incalculably better place, if only the Greeks had had a word for it?

Just the Ticket

It was a familiar enough sight in Park Lane, at two o'clock in the morning. It was what you would have expected to see.

I was leaning on my new garden fork, and I was holding a pair of tartan knickers, a plaster Dalmatian with an illuminable head, and a jeroboam of some thick yellow fluid which the picture on the label encouraged me to believe had been distilled from persimmons, although I had to take this somewhat on trust, my Serbo-Croat being what it is.

The woman beside me, who was cradling a set of cricket

81

stumps, an electric blanket, and what appeared to be a kit for assembling the Forth Bridge out of coat-hangers, glanced at my bottle and said:

"You'll like that, we drank a lot of that in Dubrovnik last year. Or was it Izmir?"

"I really couldn't say," I replied.

"The boat went everywhere. You lost track after a bit. What I do know is that the place we drank it, they had money with holes in. Do they call that a magnum?"

"It's a jeroboam, actually," I said.

At this point, a chap I know came by without a fairy cycle.

"Where's your fairy cycle?" I enquired.

"I got fifty quid for it," he said. The lamps of old Mayfair lit his eyes with that radiance which only comes from turning a 500 per cent profit while the rest of the world is snoring. He passed on, chortling, his plastic bag of Waterford decanters tinkling in his wake.

"Fancy," said the woman. "Do people do that?"

"Some do," I said. "It goes on. I myself got a snorkel that way, once."

"What's a jeroboam?" said the woman, after a bit.

"A mighty man of valour who made Israel to sin," I said. "Kings, I think. Possibly Chronicles."

"No, I mean seriously," said the woman.

A cab slowed, but carried on. Who could blame it? A lot of people are looking for cabs at 2am; you can earn a living without stopping for every drunk in an unravelled bow who waves a garden fork at you.

"It's four bottles," I said. I looked at it. The contents had the iridescence of a contaminated cistern. I felt my dinner move slightly.

"Nearly a gallon," I said.

"I wonder what it would cost?" said the woman.

The chap without the fairy cycle came back, slightly unsteadily.

"Look at this!" he cried. "It's got four wavebands and it makes tea. Silly arse couldn't wait to get rid of it."

"What did you give him?" I said.

"Can't tell you," he said. "You'll only start accusing me of something."

He loped on, into the darkness. I hefted the bottle, to see if it had a price-tag, but it didn't; mind you, even if it had, who knew how many coins with holes in there were to the pound, these days?"

"All I know is," I said, "it cost me a tenner."

"So did this," said the woman, quickly. "All the tickets were the same price. Mine's probably worth three times that."

I looked at the coat-hanger kit.

"What is it?" I said.

"It's a wrought-iron hanging basket. It can take up to nine pot plants. I know that, because we've already got one, unfortunately. You could not believe the difference it makes to a patio. Or," she added, "balcony."

A minute or two passed, before my wife shimmied out of Grosvenor House looking like a woman a cabbie would drive to the ends of the earth, and held up a hand. I crept across, and got in.

"I'll have that wossname, fork, up here with me," said the cabbie.

We collapsed into the seats.

"What's that thing?" she said.

"It's a hanging basket," I said. "It takes nine pots."

"Oh God," she said. "I didn't see you win a hanging-basket. Couldn't you swop it for anything?"

"Don't you think that sort of defeats the tombola spirit?"

"No," she said. She poked among the plastic bags. "Where's that nice big bottle of whatever-it-is?"

Nobody Likes a Swat

Have they gone yet? Can I relax?

Theirs is, thank God, a short season. Now that the globe is warmer, it starts on the same day as pheasant (October 1), and it is over, usually, in a fortnight. Were it to end on the same day as pheasant (February 1), I should emigrate. This is because a further dissimilarity with pheasant is that you can kill pheasant. You cannot kill these.

Or, rather, you may not. There would be no problem killing them if you were allowed to. I know this because you used to be allowed to, and it was a lot easier than pheasant. Also a lot cheaper. You did not require a pair of matched Purdeys and a hollow shooting-stick full of Glenlivet, you did not have to climb into thermal underwear or a Range Rover, you needed the services of neither a bloke with an expensive retainer to flush your quarry out, nor a labrador with an expensive pedigree to cart your quarry in.

All you needed was a pair of matched rolled-up newspapers. You needed two because you had to have a spare so that you were always ready, and once you had used the first, you did not want to use it again. You did not even want to look at it again. This was because after you had used it, and the quarry was dead, you discovered just how much quarry there had been. Spread out and separated into its various components, there was ten times more of it than there had ever been in life. It is a characteristic it has in common with the artichoke, though considerably more horribly.

Sportsmen among you will have by now identified the crane-fly, known popularly as *tipula paludosa*, but to scientists as daddy-longlegs. Any of its names will, I know, have stirred that dormant heyday in the blood that used to bubble up each autumn at the first faint but unmistakable tapping at the ceiling, calling keen-eared hunters from cot and fauteuil, whence, with piercing cries of "The game's a-foot!", we should be off and running, now scaling the sideboard, now trampolining the mattress for the airborne flail, now dropping to all fours to despatch the merely stunned as they zig-zagged the shagpile with all the pluck and cunning of their kind.

The game which was afoot was a working-class game. It was what we had instead of ptarmigan and kudu. And, like all true huntsmen, we gave not a hoot that our quarry was neither enemy nor food: the chase was all. And the beast enjoyed it; how could it not! Its natural life was but 12 hours: bound by ruthless nature to the briefest nookie, it did not even get a square meal before it declined into doddering dotage. Better by far not to go gentle into that good night, but to hop about a bit, before the *TV Times* despatched you, in your fighting prime! And often to give as good as you got, as the hunter barked his shins or, swiping, swept a cherished heirloom from his mantelpiece.

Hemingway would have understood. Indeed, until I made the mistake of reading it, I believed that the eponym of *The Short Happy Life of Francis Macomber* was a particularly collectable species of tipulosa which Papa had managed to bring down with his .44 Springfield.

There are, after all, 320 species. I know this because the Nature Conservancy Council has said so, enjoining us not to swat any of them because they are already endangered by more than tightly rolled Business Sections.

This has given me a bad fortnight: my wife is not merely not the kind of woman who shrieks when a room fills with dangling legs, thus giving her protector an excuse to ignore the NCC, she is also living with the kind of protector who shrieks when a room fills with dangling legs.

For two weeks now, I have had tipulosa groping for my head, dancing on my reading material, flitting over my soup, and appearing in my favourite television programmes. Even though they brought welcome comic relief to the undraped writhings of *Portrait of a Marriage*, this has been a grisly time. And the thought that I have done my bit for a conservation which might well ensure that there are twice as many of them next year brings, oddly enough, scant consolation.

The Drainman Cometh

Y ou will say I encourage him. My wife says I encourage him. My daily says I encourage him. My neighbours say I encourage him.

And I would say I encourage him, if I felt it was the right word for what I do to him. But courage is the last thing he needs. If you spend your life tramping up garden paths and banging on doors and shouting through windows, thereby enfranchising the respectable to dig deep into their repertoire of expletives, set their dogs on you, and require of the local police force an explanation of why they pay their taxes, you already have more courage than you can shake a stick at; which is why, when sticks are shaken at him, he merely takes one pace backwards and launches into a supplementary monologue about gullies.

For he is the Drainman. That is why I do what I do to him, which is not encourage, but, I suppose, cherish. He is the last survivor of that shuffling line whose disappearance has also put out of business those craftsmen who used to make small enamel signs. You do not, these days, see gate-posts warning off hawkers, tinkers, pedlars, knife-grinders, and all those other itinerant botchers who, in the sweet lang syne, used to stand on the doorstep repairing saucepans with little metal discs which melted the first time you lit the gas beneath them, or fitting broomhandles with new brushes which fell off immediately they confronted major dust.

I miss them. They brought a whiff of rurality to peripolitan life, they helped blur the edges between grass and concrete. Were there a Council for the Preservation of Suburban England, they would be subsidized to carry on wandering about and cocking things up.

As it is, here in Cricklewood only the Drainman remains. He appeared this morning, as I guessed he might, because autumn had suddenly struck and there was wind to blow the leaves off and rain to pulp them. I knew it was him as soon as the knocker banged: he is the only caller who uses the knocker. Everyone else rings the bell, but the Drainman recognizes that, in 1990, the knocker is nothing but the nod which decor makes towards nostalgia, and he embraces the pretence, because he knows that such appeal as he has lies in being part of it.

"I've been round," he said, as I opened the door, "and you wouldn't credit it. Full of acacia everywhere. Get acacia spoliage into the system, and you are in serious trouble."

Spoliage is one of his words. It is a great word. It exists nowhere else. That is another feature of the Drainman: he has, just as all professions do, endowed his trade with the exclusivity of jargon.

"Know what this is?" he said, as I followed him into the scything rain. I looked at it. It was a metal coathanger, or had been, once.

"It is a downpipe-reamer," he said. "They have to be made up special. They are the only things for deblocking solidified grit. They would give their eye-teeth for these up Dyno-rod."

We bent over a grating.

"It all seems to be running away all right," I said.

"Oh, I'm not saying it's not running away all right *now*," he said. "That is why I am here. Timing is everything in my profession. It'll be a different story tomorrow. You would not believe the speed of acacia, with the wind in the east."

"It's in the north," I said.

"At the moment it is," he said. "I know wind. You have to, in this game. Anyway, it's the north wind brings bird's nests down. Get a bird's nest in your Y-trap, you could be looking at a whole new system. Luckily, I brought this." He dug into a pocket of his enormous greatcoat, and produced a bottle of viscous brown fluid. "Nest solvent," he said. "Made to a secret formula. I have been offered a fortune for it."

I left him to get on with it. I always do. Tomorrow, the drive will be under water, and after I have rolled my sleeves up and soaked my knees, I shall almost certainly find a twisted coathanger blocking a drain, or a thrombosis coagulated to a secret formula forcing a cataract from a length of newly dislodged guttering. But I shan't really mind.

By Their Fruits Ye Shall Know Them

It is that time of year when the trees in my front garden appear to be full of strawberries. It is an astonishing sight; a colour plate from one of those *mitteleuropaische* folderols in which two winsome tots wander into the forest and fetch up at such stuff as pick-your-own dreams are made on, little knowing it to be the bait set by a witch with a couple of vacancies in her pie-dish.

My trees are 15ft high, and heavy with fruit. You could reach out from my bedroom window and pluck the topmost. Were you to do so, mind, you would very soon discover that they were not strawberries at all; especially if you bit into one. They are Fools' Strawberries. Films set in the Cricklewood of 1849 teem with old-timers sniggering at tenderfoot prospectors who hurtle into town and leap from their mules shrieking that the hills are full of soft fruit just waiting to be picked up. I have, indeed, heard it mooted that these are in fact the crickles of which the original wood was composed, and until such time as a more authoritative etymology turns up, I am happy to believe it.

The botanical term for these flora, however, is arbutus, and in addition to the stunning similarity of their offspring to strawberries, they are remarkable in that they produce blossom and fruit simultaneously, which is about as close to wantonness as a plant can get. Were they women, tongues would not stop wagging. In fact, it is precisely this gamey mix of lust and motherhood which enables them to have two seasons per annum, and drive birds barmy in April as well as in October.

What drives them barmy is that while arbutus fruit give every appearance of juicy beaksomeness, they not only taste horrible, their scarlet hulls consist of minuscule spheres of grit held together by superglue, the effects of which is to fill the garden with jays and chaffinches frenziedly stropping their bills on twig and fencepost. That they have never learnt to distinguish between the strawberry and its unsavoury simulacrum must be put down to the fact that birds have very small brains which do not develop; otherwise, I suppose, they would have evolved into greengrocers.

Imagine, therefore, my astonishment yesterday morning, when, the darkness not yet fully ebbed, I looked out of my bedroom window and saw two ancient ladies with a black plastic bag strung between them, plucking my fruit from the boughs that overhung the road. A rather pleasing sight, actually, the misty dawn, the laden trees, the two toiling biddies, all framed within the sash: it was like having John Everett Millais's *The Arbutus-Pickers* hanging on your bedroom wall.

But it could not be left at that. Who could bear the thought of these two old dears, after all their septuagenarian effort, gleefully emptying their trophies into their little porringers, only to discover the nauseating truth? Spending the rest of the day banging their dentures against the wall in the pitiful attempt to dislodge a thousand gummy pips? I threw open the window.

They took off like whippets. I shrugged. What else could I do? But after I had shut the window again, my worry took a graver turn: I did not know if arbutus fruit was poisonous. Nature had after all gone to great lengths to put anyone off eating it. But were it to be doused in sugar and cream, might the old ladies not get enough down to kill them? Should I organize an all-points bulletin, phone hospitals, all that?

At 9 o'clock, I phoned Kew. The switchboard patched in the Poisons Desk. Don't worry, said the Poisons Desk, arbutus may not be edible, but it is not poisonous. I described what I had seen. The Poisons Desk thought for a bit, and said: "Might they have been Irish?"

This is Cricklewood. "Yes," I said, "why?"

"In the 16th century," said the Poisons Desk, "Irish monks began distilling a liqueur from arbutus. I believe some Irish folk still do."

I thanked her, and put the phone down. Is it not a wonderful world? More to the point, does anyone out there have the recipe? I would appear to be sitting on a goldmine.

A Sound of Revelry by Night

Little did André-Jacques Garnerin think, as he plummeted from his balloon into the shrubbery of the Parc Monceau on that brisk autumn day in 1797, that this first parachute descent would be so egregiously commemorated in Cricklewood exactly 193 years later!

The October 22 fireworks were magnificent. The welkin exploded into streak and starshell, dogs went mad, and such Old Contemptibles as still survive lurched in their cots to sudden dreams of Mons and Ypres. Good old Garnerin, to generate such fun! Unless, of course, these pyrotechnic parties were in fact being thrown for Hawley Crippen, convicted on that selfsame date in 1910. I have asked around, but could elicit only the even more confusing opinion that the jumping jacks were hopping about in celebration of the birthday of Sarah Bernhardt.

October 23's display, though, was unquestionably ignited on behalf of the Battle of Edgehill. Cricklewood makes no secret of its bi-cultural cruces, and any appearance in the calendar of Oliver Cromwell is always good for a commemorative detonation or two down here. The bombardment of October 24 was, however, more inponderable: I doubt that the villagers would have forked out for either Zambia's National Day or the signature of the Treaty of Westphalia, and I am only guessing when I say that the 1945 execution of Vidkun Quisling must have made more of a local impression than one had hitherto assumed.

91

But no such doubts attached to the historical provenance of all the rocket sticks that fell in my garden on the night of October 25. Beyond question, these showered down in homage to the longbowed arrows that saved Cricklewood's bacon at Agincourt; and how could one grumble at the morrow's need to pluck them from pond and gutter, when a moment's reflection reminded me that, but for the immemorial doings of St Crispin's Day, I should probably be grumbling in French?

But how to explain, on Friday, a sudden nocturnal barrage with which any Second Front would have been proud to open? While my wife got up to put the kettle on, I groped for the encyclopaedia, to find that nothing of celebratory moment had happened on October 26, save the birth of François Mitterrand and the opening of the Erie Canal. But hardly had I plumped for the latter – on the grounds that since it had been dug entirely by Irishmen, their Cricklewood descendants would not let a million ancestral callouses go uncommemorated – than my wife, who is something of a soccer fanatic, pointed out that it was, in fact, the 127th anniversary of the Football Association.

Hers must be the correct attribution. Furthermore, I have to conclude, from the niffy detritus of expended thunderflashes which next morning littered the front garden, that a hooligan element cannot be ruled out.

We were out on Saturday night, but the gauntlet we drove back through bore witness that the agglomerated births of Captain Cook, Niccolo Paganini, Dylan Thomas, Theodore Roosevelt, Glen Hoddle and, of course, John Cleese did not go unrecorded by the neighbourhood's touch-papers.

There was a particular poignancy to Sunday night's explosions. Because it was exactly 87 years since the birth of Evelyn Waugh three streets from mine at 11 Hillfield Road, and because the poor chap had spent the rest of his life attempting to conceal that he was a son of Cricklewood, the sound the sensitive ear could detect beneath the crack and sizzle was the pitiable noise of a snob turning in his grave at posterity's refusal to disclaim on his behalf what he had steadfastly refused to claim in his own. Still, the fact that what was lit were Roman candles may have gone some way towards appeasing his proselytized shade.

It is Monday as I write, and already the air is acrid with the recognition of the founding of the Red Cross. At least, I hope it is; the alternative is the birth of Goebbels. And there is much more to come, I know, before November 4 – though why that should be the date the season traditionally closes, I have never been certain. It may, I suppose, simply be that unhappy day on which the historians run out of ammunition.

NOVEMBER

Fabric Conditioning

I sat next to Peter Palumbo a year or so ago, at one of those nominally informal bunfights where "Just a Few Close Friends" is hand-scribbled on the embossed paste board, and when you get there two liveried footmen shuck you from your Pakamac and the third shouts your name into a room containing most of the *Almanack de Gotha*, half the cabinet, and a shoal of tycoons not yet on remand, and you immediately begin asking yourself what your host thinks it is you've got that one of his other guests wants, because you were not born yesterday.

Anyway, Palumbo was an agreeable enough cove, he didn't spill anything on me or try that trick with the cutlery where you bang the spoon and the fork does a somersault, and I was therefore not surprised to learn, a few months later, that he had been made chairman of the Arts Council; if you keep going to informal dinners with Just a Few Friends night after night, and don't knock over the potted palms, you have only yourself to blame when the scrap of paper that unexpectedly falls out of your hat in the homegoing Roller turns out to have a black spot on it.

Especially if you cannot forbear from banging on publicly about the Cultural Fabric of the Nation: it is the one phrase of his I recall from that night's exchanges, and each time he loosed it, I rose snapping to the fly, ticking off the threat to that fabric, i.e., to theatre, film, music, books, painting – and, by Stilton time, to glove-puppetry and synchronized origami – from the Philistine hordes yomping behind a Delilah whose manic shears were cutting everything in sight. Palumbo's eyes would glaze excitedly at each new convoluted metaphor, oddly like those of a man attempting to remember a previous engagement, but whether my shafts were scoring it was not only impossible to say, it did not really matter, since I had no idea, then, that he would ever be in a position to do anything about them.

Indeed, the meeting lay forgotten until I opened last Friday's *Times*, where, lurking at the foot of page 5, was the phrase "the Arts Council's plan to restore the cultural fabric of the nation by the year 2000". Hallo, I thought, its new Akela cleaves unswerving to his mission, there will be a bob or two in this for hack and mummer, might I not be of even further assistance than last time? I phoned the Arts Council.

"This cultural fabric," I said, "what, precisely, does it . . ."

"To quote the chairman," said the Arts Council, "cathedrals are the greatest cultural glory of this country. He plans to refurbish their fabric by means of a full partnership between the public and private sectors. Other major public buildings, too, of course . . ."

I put the phone down. Bloody buildings. The man had not listened to a word I'd shrieked. He was a literalist: to him, fabric was no metaphor. New conks for gargoyles was what he was after, and a bit of Brasso on the weathercock. Naturally, the private sector would cough up for that: there is nothing iffy about a cathedral, shareholders will not leap up at AGMs and complain about chucking a million at York Minster. On the contrary, it is no bad thing for a board to be seen as God's benefactors, it is a corking plea in mitigation should their hands get trapped in the till, it has a thick edge over backing unframed paintings or unrhymed verse or unknighted actors.

And what irks me almost as much is that, even for the literalist, cathedrals should top the list when our cultural fabric is under charitable review. Someone will always look after cathedrals. Had I identified, that night, the true bee in Palumbo's bonnet, I should have turned myself into the Spirit of Cultural Fabric Yet to Come, dragged him down to Cricklewood, made him cringe at butchered conversion and greenfield encroachment, at junkfood facia and bunkered parking, at jerrycobbled estate and polystyrene precinct; I should have cocked his ear to the curfew tolling the knell of parting suburbia.

Bit late now. The window of opportunity has slammed, and one of the very few shortcomings of mock-mullioned double-glazing in snugfit cedarette surround is you can't hear anyone shouting through it.

Odour-Nicer Lines

Something truly astonishing happened last Sunday. Something not only extraordinary in itself but so pregnant with implication that, five days on, the brain still reverberates like a Sumerian battle-gong. Because last Sunday, for one brief but glorious moment, my entire peer group smelt exactly the same! Suddenly we were, as that dear departed dandy Leonard Sachs might have cried had he been here to dab the stuff on, a fraternity of fragrance, an aristocracy of aroma, nay, a pantheon of parfumerie!

99

And what did we smell of? We smelt of exotic trees: 630,000 of us. A whole exotic forest. A Metropolitan Matto Grosso. I knew it was my peer group, because the 630,000 were all London and Home Counties readers of *The Sunday Times*. That is how many copies of its regional Fashion Supplement were distributed, and that, therefore, is how many sachets of Givenchy Gentleman reached the doormats, and thence the cheeks, of Britain's most favoured corner.

Do not query that "thence". I have been about a bit, and just as I know that the man is yet unborn who, walking into an unoccupied room containing a hat, will not try it on, I know that if a free sachet of eau de toilette is gummed to the page of a magazine, it is only a matter of time before a man will tug it off, rip it open, and slosh it over himself. That is the way the world is, otherwise Givenchy would not have sat up day and night squirting tiny amounts of Gentleman into little silver envelopes. Furthermore, lest you take me for an insouciant *siffleur*, I have done my research: I have worked out that if each sachet contained its declared 1.5 millilitrés, then Givenchy had committed 945 litres to this exercise, or 207 gallons for those who have forgotten we are now in the ERM, or, for those others who have trouble with statistics, the fuel-tank capacity of five London buses, which, by anyone's standards, is a lot of Gentleman.

So much for what I know. It is time to address what I do not know. First, I do not know how Givenchy arrived at the conclusion that gentlemen want to smell of Gentleman. I offer this from the sachet's shimmering rubric: "Classed as a woody aromatic fragrance, Givenchy Gentleman is distinctive with its force of leather notes, in harmony with exotic woods." You will agree that it is not entirely clear whether it will make you smell like an Amazonian tree-dweller in a rancid thong, or a bloke who spends all day selling teak-and-leather furniture, but whichever it is, what persuaded Givenchy that a gentleman would wish to exude the impression of being either?

Especially in view of what Givenchy believes he is – "the man who is totally at ease in today's world" in search of "an untamed, vigorous and intense fragrance for the bolder provocative man of action". Those of us unversed in the arcane ways of aromatics might be forgiven for thinking, might we not, that were you a bold provocative man of action totally at ease in today's world, the last thing that would concern you was your odour? In our ignorance, we might have felt you wouldn't care if you gave off the untamed, vigorous and intense fragrance of a camel.

But, I asked myself last Sunday, did Givenchy – which was after all putting its money where its mouth was – know better? Might its expensive research in fact have thrown up 630,000 bold, provocative, confident Home Counties men of action, strung out from Amersham to the Straits of Dover, eager to reek of sap and tannin? And was that not a heady thought, particularly in patriotic heads still rattling with uncertainties about hitching their wagon to the Bundesbank star?

Boldly, provocatively, confidently, I splashed it on. How good it felt, pledging one's membership of that great army! True, the day passed without anyone remarking upon either my totality of ease or my egregiousness of action, as a matter of fact they didn't even sniff and say, "Am I wrong, or is there an exotic tree in here?", but no matter, I know what I know. Which is that, should our services ever be called upon, there are 630,000 of us who will not shrink from commanding the world to watch the wall, my darlings, as the Gentleman runs by.

Nothing But The Truth

If a man spends 30 years banging a key for money, it must follow that not everything he writes will come up to impeccable snuff.

There will be up days and down days, there will be up markets and down markets, but if hot meals are to be set upon tables and carpets laid upon floorboards, if pipes are to be professionally plumbed and cats professionally wormed, and if children are not to be dispatched barefoot to school (perhaps for no better reason than to escape the spectacle of their mother taking in washing at the back door even as the bailiffs at the front are distraining upon their father's chattels), then, willy-nilly, the loin must be girt and, though the *mots* may not always be *justes*, the quota filled.

Yet if those three decades have therefore spewed much of which I was not proud, they had not, until yesterday, delivered anything of which I was actually ashamed. But when I recall yesterday's *oeuvre*, it pumps the blood into the cheeks, even as the pump itself plummets to the bottom of the boots. Worse, yesterday I put my name to a piece of writing which could settle my professional hash for good.

Its plot was generated some nights earlier, when the next-door burglar alarm sounded. This did not greatly agitate me, since it is a capriciously sensitive item and had doubtless responded to a raindrop or a coughing dog, but I went into the front garden to check – one of my dahlias might have fallen over – whereupon the lamp-light revealed a man paused at my neighbour's gate. Had this passer-by spotted something? I ran back, phoned the police, and ran out again with the idea of asking the man what he had seen.

It now dawned on me that what he had seen was the inside of the house, because he was disappearing up the road at a clip too nimble to be innocent. I clipped after, but before I could close upon him he darted into the unlit playing-fields opposite, and there is an age beyond which you do not follow the unknown into the invisible. Fortunately, even as my *amour propre* seeped, a police car hurtled around the corner, flung open its rear door at my wave, and we plunged together in a pursuit which happily ended at the quarry's collar.

As the result of which, I was of course required to make a statement. That I was not required to make it immediately was, I felt, all to the good: recollecting emotion in tranquillity means you can marshal a few smart adjectives and get the semi-colons right. Accordingly, when the CID amanuensis fronted up yesterday, I was ready. He opened his pad, I my mouth, and we set off together towards the Booker Prize.

I had never dictated a story before. Habituated to pecking syllables off a keyboard in between staring out of the window, I had not realized how wonderfully the mind was concentrated by sitting opposite a bloke with a big fat pad and an urgent ballpoint. The stuff poured out.

It was pretty good: true, there was a nod to Wilkie Collins, a whiff of Chandler, but it was in the main my own, and it rattled along a treat. As the policeman scribbled, I thought, this is a watershed, I could do trilogies, I wonder if he'd like to earn a bob or two on his day off?

We finished, and he passed the pad across. Was it, he enquired, a true record of the facts, would I sign it to this effect, would I attend court?

I read it. I said yes. It came out as a croak. For, though every fact was true, every embellishment had gone. The copper was as remarkable an editor as I had ever met. As he wrote, he subbed: it is a great art, though that is not what it produces. It produces *Janet and John*.

Soon, I shall be in court. Defence counsel rises. His client is alleged to have been caught bang to rights. His only course is to discredit the witness. He settles his gold pince-nez. He reads. "I saw a man. The man was at the gate. The man had a brown jacket. He ran up the road. I ran after him. I got quite close. The man had little ears. The man ran across the road. I ran . . ."

Defence counsel tosses the sheaf aside, and takes off his pince-nez. "Mr Coren, you have described yourself to this court, under oath, as a writer . . ."

Sits the Wind in that Corner?

Can it really be but one short week since Englishmen were running around their gardens, crying: "How horrible, fantastic, incredible it is, that we should be digging trenches and trying on balaclavas here because of a deep depression over a far-away ocean between two occluded fronts of which we know nothing?"

Strange it was, that Pre-Wind period. I did not myself dig any trenches, having replaced all my fences after the Last Lot, thereby obviating the need, when storm clouds once more threatened this island race, to sink concrete stanchions as per my esteemed order, bolt 4x4 uprights thereto, attach 20 lengths best feather-boarding, creosote and make good to highest finish, remove all rubbish from site and go bank-rupt. But all around me, last Friday, the gardens rang with the noise of spade on kneecap as frantic neighbours dug in against the imminent onslaught.

I did, however, a lot of battening down. Who dared not,

given the hourly alarums of Met Office windmongers still stinging, three years on, from meteorology's Pearl Harbour? Quite how far up the mobility-scale to batten was another matter; clearly, notes should not be placed in milk-bottles, nor even milk-bottles on steps, but how about, say, crated milk-bottles? Should crates be lashed to gates? Or dustbins: since the First Great Hurricane, when lids flew like Frisbees, our old bins had all been replaced by wheelies. True, their lids were attached, but who could assess their potential for instability? Might they, when the typhoon struck, begin to roll? Was our hill looking at a Sorcerer's Apprentice situation? But if we moved our kerbside cars out of the way of the hurtling charge, it could only be back into the driveways from which we had already moved them out of the way of the falling slates.

How much of a tree should one lop? Was it riskier to crawl out and rope a dodgy chimney than to let the bricks fall where they may? Should hanging baskets merely be lowered to the ground and left, or brought indoors against the possibility that they might gradually rock themselves across the lawn and through the lower panes of the greenhouse? What of the greenhouse iteslf – did one open its doors to prevent the wind's shattering it, or shut them to prevent the wind's blowing everything that was inside outside?

You did what you could, you went to bed, and you lay awake, ears cocked and trembling for the blitz. You did this three nights on the trot. But nothing happened. It was the Phoney Wind. On Monday, the Met Office confirmed that no blue birds had been blown over the white cliffs of Dover. Johnny could sleep in his own little room again. You were no longer advised to tether him to the boiler.

The days grew so calm and sunny, indeed, that I decided to paint the front door. I had been planning this for some time, but the propitious moment had not hitherto offered itself. Now it had. We had come through. The door that might have blown off had not even been invited to rattle. A celebration was required.

The paint went on a treat: when I stood back at last, the finish was irreproachable. So smooth, so lustrous, that, were a vacancy suddenly to occur in the ranks of Joan Collins's *maquillage* team, I could have taken the door round as a reference. Leaving it to dry, I went in and poured myself a congratulatory Scotch. As I did so, the latch of the back door rattled. I looked through the window, but there was no one there. While I was looking out, a leaf flew in, and then another. The back door rattled again, and blew open.

By the time I got to the front door it resembled nothing so much as a kindergarten nature-table. There were sycamore seeds stuck to it, and little berries and a variety of insects so catholic as to whet even the most jaded entomological palate. I got the bumblebee off, because it was still in working nick, and as it flew away I could not forbear a sneer at a creature so dumb as not to appreciate the risk of being blown into a freshly painted door.

Fancy not knowing that a wind can suddenly come up out of nowhere.

Will Power

Yes, since you ask, it was a very busy weekend indeed. I spent the whole of it rewriting my will.

I suppose I should amplify that terse announcement, if only to settle the fluttering breasts of those who might believe themselves to be my legatees, and who are even now muttering, blimey, that has to be some will, it has taken him two days to rewrite it, he must have more than anyone guessed, I always thought there was something a bit fly about him, I wonder who gets the chain of casinos, I wonder who gets the Reeperbahn flophouses, I wonder who gets the uncatalogued Van Goghs and the lost dinner service of Tutankhamun?

Forget it. It was not the rewriting that took the weekend, it was the rereading of that with which the rewriting was concerned. I have been going through my unpublished works. I have been sorting them out into teetering piles. I have been putting them into cardboard boxes. Only when that was done did I rewrite the will.

You will, I know, have been following the Larkin *cause macabre*. How could you have missed it? For weeks, not only have the casements of Fitzrovia rattled to the din of grinding axes, the furore has spilled over into every public print and on to every public channel, as those who have never read a line of poetry throw their two penn'orth into the posthumous tussle between an unacknowledged legislator of the world and the battalions of acknowledged ones, I shall say nothing of that, since so much has already been said that the words expended on whether Larkin wanted his unpublished stuff destroyed now considerably outnumber the words of his published stuff, and anyway, this is about me.

Perhaps nothing so distinguishes the poet from the hack as his attitude towards his unpublished work. The poet's attic is full of stuff he wouldn't publish, the hack's only of stuff he couldn't. For one thing, there is never anything a hack is so ashamed of writing that it prevents him from seeking someone who is not ashamed of publishing it, and for another, while the poet's diddy-boxes are crammed with letters, notebooks, diaries, well-turned suicide notes for such deployment as future despair might require and various other private scribblings, all of which stand testament to man's need to express the innermost churnings of his soul, the hack's have nothing in them except those agglomerations of correspondence and invoice which stand testament only to man's need to keep the wolf at the far end of the garden path.

For the hack is disinclined to squander time on private epistle and journal which might be more profitably spent in cobbling a piece for *Plumbing Today*, or, indeed, a smarmy note to the Inland Revenue anent the deductability of new fitted carpet without which the productivity of creative premises might be seriously impaired. Yet the hack, too, yearns as much as the poet for posthumous bonus: it is not, of course, the prospect of immortality that moves him, merely the thought of leaving stuff behind that could be parlayed for a bob or two.

I do not claim that my boxes of unmarketable typescript will bring literary scholars cart-wheeling down the pavements, nor that my long and fascinating correspondence with Lex Volvo will change the face of epistolary history as we know it (since Lex Volvo is not a fashionable Latin-American novelist but simply the organization which supplied an estate car with an apparently irreparable clunk), but I have nevertheless taken steps to ensure that all this and more will, after I am dead, appear between remunerative hard covers.

I have inserted a clause in my will insisting that all my unpublished work be published. I have specified the publisher, who, I am utterly confident, will be unable to wriggle free of the paramount wishes of the deceased without a legal cost to himself considerably in excess of the advances I have taken pains to calculate and demand.

Not, I guess, that he will want to. Why, with a modicum of luck, the juridical barney alone should flog a good few copies.

Top Secret

Remember *Rear Window*? James Stewart, immobilized by nether plaster and forced to while away the time peering out at the premises opposite, one day spots Raymond Burr behaving oddly and convinces himself that no good is being got up to. Naturally enough, this being Hitchcock, Stewart has great difficulty convincing anyone else, and it is not until the spottee spots himself being spotted and lumbers round to knock his spotter off that the police accept that all is not as it should be chez Burr and start dusting down the electric chair.

The scene now shifts to a Cricklewood attic, where a hack immobilized by professional sterility (a condition whose symptoms, indeed, closely resemble having your brain in plaster) is forced to while away the time peering out at the premises opposite. On one such morning, he spots two men perched on a roof. They are not up to no good, but they are not up to good, either. They are not up to anything. They are just up.

The hack watched them climb up, three hours earlier, and since they were carrying tool bags, it was reasonable to assume that they had been commissioned to service the roof. True, the hack had, as well as *Rear Window*, also seen *Rififi* and *Topkapi*, but he did not believe the two men were international jewel thieves bent on forcing entry through the roof, because he could not recall a scene in either *Rififi* or *Topkapi* where the international jewel thieves spent two hours setting

109

up an external hoist, swearing noisily at one another, and whistling at everything that shimmied past below.

There was, of course, always the off-chance that this was a sly diversionary tactic, but the way in which the third hour was spent allayed even this remote suspicion. The hack could not recall a scene in either *Rififi* or *Topkapi* where the international jewel thieves produced a gas stove, cooked breakfast, ate it, and, having finished the *Sun*, started playing cards.

An hour later, the two men climbed down again, and rattled off in their Transit. They rattled back at around 2pm, reclimbed their ladder, spent 10 minutes securing a large polythene sheet over the roof, and the next hour lying on it. At 3.30 they got up, prised half a dozen tiles from the roof, threw them into the hoist's bucket, and put the kettle on. Sensible men both, they knew they needed something hot inside them for the journey home, which, soon after four, they took.

By tea on the following day – which had followed the self-same pattern, except that valuable brag-time did not have to be eaten into by laying down polythene sheets – the hack was growing somewhat irritated. Though his life was spent pecking at a garret keyboard, his was not a bohemian but a bourgeois spirit, and the fact that, opposite, a fair day's pay was not buying a fair day's work got right up his nose. Furthermore, he had had men on his own roof from time to time, and recalled, now, that corrosive mix of suspicion and impotence which accompanies the relationship between folding money and unobservable work. The men could not be seen by their client below; they could not be seen by anyone except the hack. Should he interfere?

The third day exacerbated his dilemma. No tiles got thrown into the bucket at all. The hack passed the entire morning wrestling with both his conscience and his self-image, for he liked snoopers as little as he liked layabouts. Nor, it must be said, did he much like the idea of two roofers coming round and knocking him off. What would James Stewart have done? James Stewart had, after all, long been the custodian of moral probity and community spirit. The hack looked up his neighbour's phone number. After a bit, he picked up the telephone.

It was even as he dialled that one of the roofers looked across, waved at him, and grinned. Involuntarily, the hack waved back. Then he put the phone down. Something had happened. The fellowship of the roof. More yet: had the roofers been watching the hack for three days, asking themselves why he never did a stroke? Let him who is without sin chuck the first tile in the bucket.

Poor old Raymond Burr. He could so easily have got away with it. All he had to do was wave.

DECEMBER

Change and Decay

There's not a lot of things Michael Caine doesn't know, but I am willing to bet that one of them is that a cigar-box holds exactly £7. In fact, I am willing to bet £7 that he doesn't. I know where I can lay my hands on that precise sum. You will say: hang on, he might just *say* that he knows, and how can you prove that he doesn't? If you do, I shall reply that if he does know, he will also know how much a cigar-box containing £7 weighs, because if you knew the one you would know the other. There's not a lot of people know that.

I single our Mr Caine for this public wager not simply because he is the national repository of statistical arcana, but also because he is a cigar-smoker, and I am a gambler. True gamblers take no pleasure in racing certainties; they prefer to give a sucker an even break, else where's the thrill? Though there is only a remote possibility that Michael hangs on to his old cigar-boxes, and an even remoter one that, when he empties his trouser-pockets of an evening, he throws his copper coins into one of them, a possibility there is.

After all, I do. Or, more precisely, I have been doing for the past year. I started because I had an empty cigar-box, and I find it impossible to throw away an empty cigar-box. Nothing looks more useful. Nothing might come in handier. In consequence, I now have a large number of full cigar-boxes, in which I keep things that are less useful than cigar-boxes and might otherwise have been thrown away. There is, for example, one full of nutless bolts, and another full of boltless nuts, a pleasing symmetry of uselessness lying at the bottom of the tea-chest in which I keep all my cigar-boxes. (It was a big day when the tea-chest arrived. Unable to throw away such a useful-looking item, I stared at it for a long time before I suddenly realized that it was the best thing there was for keeping cigar-boxes in.)

Last November, my latest cigar-box fell vacant; but I had nothing to put in it. My single cuff-links, my old watch-straps, my huge collection of two-pin plugs, sidelined by rewiring, which would be invaluable if we were ever re-rewired, all these and more already had their boxes. And then I remembered that my bedside drawer was full of pennies.

Not only did they look wonderful in their new box, they represented a major breakthrough. Individually useless, they would become useful by agglomeration: never had a cigar-box been handier. I do not think I have ever spent a happier year.

Nor ended one as unhappily. Two days ago, I tried to add a pocketful of copper, but the box wouldn't take it. It was time to tot up. I emptied it onto the kitchen table, and made little piles of ten. They came, remarkably, to exactly 70. Who would have thought that seven quid could look so much? I scooped them back in the box, and drove to the bank.

There I stood in the queue with my cigar-box. When I got to the window, the teller looked at it. He looked at me. He did not start telling.

"There's seven pounds," I said.

"You'll have to bag it," he said. He slid seven little bags under his window. "Next," he said.

116

It is not easy, sitting at a table in a bank and counting out a cigarboxful of pennies. *Who is this person?* say the passing eyes. *An undemanding beggar? A talentless busker? A bogus child cashing up after Guy Fawkes week? Or just a poor sod down on his luck? Used to smoke Romeo y Julietas, but look at him now; it's a lesson to us all, no wonder Thatcher's on the way out.*

Eventually, the teller put my seven bags on the scales. That is how I know what they weighed. That is how he knew what one of them didn't.

"There's only 99p in this," he said.

Or possibly, said the eyes, *Britain's pettiest crook?*

I found it on the carpet, after a pleasant grovel, and the teller told the seven ones. My stake, Michael, if you're betting. Of course, you could always cheat by nipping up the bank with a boxful of coin to find out what it weighs, but take it from me, it isn't worth it.

For a Few Forints More

I don't know if you caught my act last Saturday. I had a pretty good crowd, because it was a pretty good act, but when you are a performer, you have to concentrate on your performance, you must not look around the audience for people you know, because if you catch their eye it can throw you. Also, the light wasn't too good. You know how it is on a November afternoon in Budapest, the sun sinks early, the fog comes up off the Danube, and before the performer knows it, the audience has begun to blend into

117

the grey, baroque backdrop. Which is why you have to have a good act. If you have a lousy act, and nobody shrieks or cheers, by about 4pm there is no way of knowing whether you have an audience at all. They might all have ambled off to watch the King of the Parrots.

We had a good act. Want to know just how good it was? By the end we had more than 600 forints in the pig. That's how good it was. These are tough times in Hungary, and nobody puts a forint in a pig unless the act is a real winner.

The pig was tied to my partner's leg. It was a small pink pig with a slot in its back, and it was luminous. Because I do not speak Hungarian, I could not ask my partner whether it was luminous so that he could see where it went if anyone tried to take advantage of the fog to cut the string and run away with it, but I didn't have to. As I say, times are tough in Hungary, and a pigful of forints is not to be sneezed at.

The King of the Parrots did not have a pig. You had to put your forint into one of his parrots. These were bolted onto his barrel-organ, another smart move, especially as the barrel-organ was bolted to his tricycle. To nick his forints, you would first have to kidnap the King of the Parrots, which is almost certainly a major offence.

Earlier, I had watched all this bolting take place. I had walked up Castle Hill, on the Buda side of the Danube, to the vast cobbled square between the Coronation Church and the Fisherman's Bastion where the citizens of Budapest promenade to watch the acts, and I had seen the King of the Parrots arrive on his tricycle. You could not tell he was a king, then, because he had not yet taken his top hat from his saddlebag, nor put on his white silk scarf and his white silk gloves, nor, of course, bolted his parrots to the barrel-organ. Then you knew. He had majesty. Psittacine, true, but majesty none the less.

He did not, however, have much of an act. The barrel organ played one tune, and the parrots' wings flapped a bit, and that was it. A thick edge over Bernard Manning, but that was about all you could say for it. After five minutes, I moved on. What I moved on to was another figure in a

118

top hat (how much capitalist millinery survived half a century of communism is another question you can't ask if you don't speak Hungarian). The second figure had not only a top hat, but a frock coat and huge clown-boots, to one of which the luminous pig was shackled. When you put a forint in his pig, he bowed, his top hat opened, and a gonk waved at you.

Minimalist stuff, but it was all he did. Until I arrived.

When I arrived, he beckoned me over. Then he mimed hat-removal, pointing at mine. I did not have a topper, but I had my brown fedora. I raised it to him. He drew me alongside. I twigged: he wanted a double act. Since it might well have been a lifetime's dream, who could refuse? He did not have much of a crowd, but the next time one of them put a forint in the pig, and the gonk waved, I raised my hat.

We were a sensation. A mob gathered. And lest you jump to the conclusion that there is not much to do in Budapest of a Saturday, let me tell you we were a class act. Synchronized swimming didn't come close. The only pity was that the partnership had to break up, but this happens in show business. Especially if one half is on a day trip to Budapest and has to get back to Gatwick.

It was a terrific day; £129 is a small price to pay for stardom.

Tangled Webs

I do not often ask your sympathy for arachnologists, but this week is different. This week, history dealt them one off the bottom of the deck. For this week was Michael Heseltine Week. But for Michael Heseltine, this would have been Peter Smithers Week.

Every morning, Mr Smithers hangs his hat at the Department of Biological Sciences, pearl in the diadem of Plymouth's Polytechnic South West; and every evening, before he puts his hat on again, he peers inside it. He also checks his raincoat pockets, his gloves, and – if it is wet – the galoshes he left in his locker. Then he shakes his scarf a couple of times, and takes a final squint in his briefcase. Mr Smithers is looking for spiders. He wants to know where they hang out. He has wanted to know this for years. That is because his life's work is *The Atlas of British Spiders*, which he does not expect to publish before 1997, since that is how long it could take to discover where the representatives of Britain's 600 species like to kick their 4,800 heels, even with me helping him.

And this was going to be the week I started, for this is the inaugural week of the National House-Spider Survey of Great Britain. Throughout the queendom, thousands of lay spider-spotters stood quivering in the slips with their little boxes, bamboo canes, and printed report forms dispatched to them by Mr Smithers. At the gun, we volunteers were to spring to our various positions beside plugholes, up curtains, under beds, behind boilers and inside cupboards, there not only to begin what was to be a year-long log of arachnoid domiciles and habits, but also to ensnare at least one example of each species clocked, pop it into a box, and post it to Plymouth for identification. For only thus would *The Atlas of British Spiders* attain the authority of Mr Smithers's dreams.

I had been looking forward to it no end. I had 10 empty fag-packets ready, an old shrimp net, a powerful torch, and a big spotted hankie to stuff in my mouth should screaming prove unavoidable. I was ready. I was keen. I was very possibly going to appear in a footnote.

It was at this point that the scene shifted suddenly to the Reichenbach Falls, upon which two figures had converged; one from the left, one from the right. They were Mr Michael Heseltine and Mrs Denis Thatcher. It was a horrible moment. Something terrible was about to happen to arachnology.

For the leadership struggle has filled the public prints.

Now, I rarely reach the shallow end of newspapers: I splash about in the deep end for a bit, allowing myself to bob up against such flotsam of pith and moment as the night's tide has washed ashore, but fatigue sets in quite early. Sated on Gulf and Gorby, I care not that cats from three counties had to be called to rescue a fireman from a tree.

But this week was different; suddenly, there was nothing up front for which I gave a fig. Indeed, the first half-dozen pages had to be avoided if one were not to find oneself trapped by an exclusive profile of the sister-in-law of a man who had once serviced Heseltine's lawn-mower, or a piece of psephological speculation on how floating Lapp Whigs might vote were Margaret Thatcher an Eskimo.

So I ignored it all, and started at page six, down-column. It was a different world. "A new problem has hit British prisons – a shortage of underpants, blamed by Mr Waddington, the Home Secretary, on vandalism." End of story. What was one to make of that? Nothing, I decided, I can forget the papers until the leadership is settled – and I was about to take up my spider-tackle and go to work, when my eye caught the story beneath. "A man who left a tarantula without food was fined £50 yesterday for causing it unnecessary suffering. Liam Conway, 22, was told by Birmingham magistrate Raymond Rider that even spiders had feelings."

You know the rest. If a beak can levy £50 on anyone making a spider peckish, what might he not do to somebody prepared to bung one in a fag packet and send it to Plymouth on a second-class stamp? Sorry, Smithers, the advancement of science is one thing, but six months in Parkhurst without underpants is quite another.

Percentage Player

Excellent, the latest *VAT Notes*. A thundering good read from start to finish, and as spiritually uplifting as anything you could shake a censer at. Those stymied for an original Yuletide gift for literary relatives would do well to consider *Leaflet No. 809696 Dd8237248 VA/D4/ 70/90*: not only is it a handy one-thousandth the length of Ackroyd's *Dickens*, its firm corners make it ideal for removing any shards of turkey still maddeningly lurking between the Boxing Day molars. And best of all, it's free – provided that you have kept up your subscription to the Customs & Excise Book Club by sending them 15% of your income every quarter.

I have had the good fortune to be a member since 1973, and have therefore received hundreds of these exegetical supplements to *The Book of VAT*. I have not, of course, been permitted to see the Book itself, for it is kept, thrice locked and acolyte-girt, in that remote forest clearing to which Brigham Excise and his followers carried it after the death of Joseph Customs (*fons et origo* of the Church of Latter-Day Taxmen), but I have been able to glean some notion of the holy text from these regular amendments. That it must be comprehensive of all that ever was since the beginning of the world is irrefutable: if the torrent of regulatory addenda can take account of such diverse minutiae as the importation of non-ferrous prostheses for ornamental (excluding clockwork) wallabies, and the exact status of purgative gherkins for ritual gatherings at which not fewer than nine of those present are full-time members of the armed forces, then it is obvious that the Book itself misses nothing. Its eye is on 115% of the sparrow.

Are the leaflets useful? It is a question as irrelevant as it is improper. They are no more or less useful than the Book of Revelations. They are not there to be useful, but to awe and mystify. They are put together by theologians concerned not merely with the number of angels able to dance on the head of a pin, but with whether the dance may be construed as educational within the meaning of the Act, enabling the pin to be zero-rated, or whether it is an entertainment, rendering the pin liable to an impost of 15%.

In this latest leaflet, for example, we read that "cigarette cards, which were formerly zero-rated, have been standard-rated since 1 September 1990". This to a world which had fully believed that cigarette cards had not been issued since Wally Hammond was No 39 in a series and Mickey Rooney was even shorter than he subsequently became. Nor was that the only window opened upon a world of which, without *VAT Notes*, we should know nothing; how many of you, for instance, realized that only the transport of passengers in a ship carrying not fewer than 12 persons was zero-rated? Does it not give a new poignancy to the cry of "Any more for the Skylark?" to appreciate that, should he dare to go round the bay with only 11 on board, the hapless skipper could well find himself clapped in Her Majesty's irons the moment his returning wellie touched the shingle?

Useful to skippers? You would have to ask a skipper, and stand out of the way. As with all holy writ, the stuff is patently there to make his life more complicated, in the hope that wrestling with its implications will be good for his soul. That is why I approach Verse 9 of the latest leaflet with due caution: there is a possibility that it is applicable to, among other merchants, purveyors of light prose to the carriage trade, but though one hand offers hope, the other offers penalty.

For Verse 9 states that "from 1 August 1990, protective boots designed for non-industrial use have been standard rated". The implications of this are obvious: it means that if the price of protective boots *designed for non-industrial use* now embraces a 15% levy, I can claim back that tax on any footwear designed to guard my feet against things falling on them while I am seated at the typewriter. This would knock nearly twelve quid off my new calf Oxfords.

Worth trying it on with the Customs & Excise scholars? Certainly. All one needs is a little faith.

Fun Fir

Once upon a time, when Fleet Street was a metonym, I drove to it every working day. Which meant that every working day – since the route from Cricklewood to solvency required me to turn from Holborn into New Fetter Lane – I spent some time at the Holborn Circus traffic lights, looking up at the buttocks of Prince Albert's horse.

Quite why this singularly unregal spot should have been chosen for the great consort's memorial I have never known (though no circus, of course, is complete without an equestrian German), but what I have always known, as the result of all this right-hand-filtering, is his dates. Because chiselled on the big granite oblong thing beneath – let us, since it is the cracker season, call it Plinth Albert – are the numbers 1819–1861.

Only 42. How came it, I would daily muse, that a fellow so sturdy and energetic (nine children and a major exhibition) should so feebly have succumbed to an exhalation from the Windsor drains? And only now am I convinced I have the clue: the clue lies in that selfsame cracker season, and the conviction lies in the conviction I risked on Wednesday for driving without due care and attention, to wit, having a dangerously uncontrollable passenger in the seat beside me.

But for Prince Albert, that passenger would have been in Norway. Albert's consuming ambition, as you know, was so to commend himself to the English that they would adopt him as their own. Not content to enjoy the unbridled passion merely of England's top banana, he sought also the adoration of her subjects. It was to this end that he imported the Christmas tree; so that, every year, the English could dance around it, breathing in its salutary needle-waft, exclaiming at its twinkling lights, clapping their hands at each spinning glass ball, cheering the topping-out of the fairy, and generally praising the name of the great benefactor.

But things did not work out that way. Instead, every year from 1841 onwards, the English stared glumly at it, wondering why its needles fell out as soon as they brought it indoors, cursing its lights for stopping twinkling the instant they stepped back to admire them, bandaging their hands at each shattered glass ball, swearing at one another for not remembering where they put the fairy last year, and generally caluminating the name of the great malefactor. Clearly, after 20 years of this, Albert's annually deepening disillusion had brought him to such a low ebb that, when the offending manhole cover was lifted, he no longer had the wherewithal to resist its miasma.

Now, until Wednesday, I had thought I had taken everything a Christmas tree could throw at me. I had believed, in short, that Prince Albert had no nasty surprises left. This was because I had never before bought a 10ft Norwegian pine at Camden Market. Too long to sit in the back seat with its head out of the window, it demanded that I put the hood down so that it could sit in front with the driver. For a time, all went well; if you ignored the hue, it was not unlike whizzing along with Isadora Duncan beside you, a big feathery thing, her tresses blowing in the slipstream, her aeolian susurrations fetchingly redolent of a wanton's murmured promises, and, the evening being crisp but not chill, I was much enjoying this, until Isadora's stays burst.

Which is to say that, on Haverstock Hill, the string restraining her limbs suddenly snapped, and, as if unable any longer to contain her vegetable lust, Isadora was all over me; so that, not merely lashed and stingingly needled, I found I could see forwards only by leaning sideways. Nevertheless, I managed; until the Panda flagged me down.

They were very good about not being in proper control of a vehicle. It was, after all, Christmas. They even had string. They rebound the tree. Only then did they notice the absence of a tax disc. We all looked at the space where it had been before, almost certainly, Isadora's outflung limb had defenestrated it. Sorry, they said, nothing we can do. Produce your documents within seven days. It's no good blaming the tree.

It's not the tree I blame, I said.

Brightly Shone The Rain That Night

B oxing Noon, and Hampstead Heath resembles nothing so much as the gale-scattered covers of all those
comic annuals ripped yestermorn from their urgent
stockings. So many bright new Mickey Mouse gloves! So
many bright new Rupert Bear scarves! So many bright new
Garfield earmuffs and Kermit boots and Peanuts pullovers!
The world, new-laminated, is crying "Hallo, Chums!"
Cavorting gaily in the drizzled gloom, all this iridescent gift-
ery – on adult and child alike – seems to bespeak not so
much Christmas as some medieval Haberdasherie Fayre
upon which the city's cordwainers and hosiers and mercers
and drapers and hatters have descended to propitiate their
diverse tutelary gods and flog their latest lines.

It is all so cartoon-jolly that I do not immediately notice
that something is missing. What makes me finally notice it
is the singularly poignant sight of a small boy sledding down
the sodden East Heath slope, towards the Vale of Health.
He has new yellow moonboots on, and a new Snoopy flying
helmet. He has a new sled. He could be on the cover of the
Beano Annual, were it not for the one thing he does not
have. He does not have snow.

Poor little begger. He is making a valiant fist of it, shoving
himself off from just beneath me, lurching down the wet
grass, slaloming the bushes with expert toe and mitten,
bumping to a halt after a dozen yards, then struggling up
again, his mudcaked sled trailing erratically behind him on

its sodden string. Had he snow, he would not stop at all, he would hurtle on, shrieking joyously, scattering the pirouetting skaters on Hampstead Pond and finally fetch up, breathless, in Gospel Oak. Because, if he had snow, there would be skaters on Hampstead Pond today, rather then the goosebumped madmen flaunting their traditional braggadocio in the unfrozen ooze.

Maybe, in his head, he has it. The imagination, at seven, is rich. Maybe he goes down the hill with six huskies in front and a pack of wolves behind. Maybe the unflagging effort is all about getting to Gospel Oak before Amundsen. My point (I have just decided) is that he shouldn't have to. He is forced to imagine only because he is forced to compensate for unnecessary disappointment. He should not have been led to expect snow. He should not have torn open his bedroom curtains, immediately after tearing open his sled-wrappings, to have his heart sunk by only drizzle specking the panes.

For two months now, cotton-wool has been his promissory note. He has stared through it at frosted toys, while Muzak jingled sleigh-bells at him. Tempted inside, he has sat on Santa's snow-booted knee, and heard how reindeer struggle through blizzards on behalf of good little boys. All his weekly reading has featured snow-capped mastheads, all the stuff within has occupied itself with snowball fights, thin ice, risible snowmen, and mad dogs happily frozen suddenly solid in the act of going for a newsboy's shin. Everything he has watched on television has ostensibly taken place in arctic conditions, and all anyone has talked about has been the prospect of the white Christmas of which he has been encouraged to dream.

No chance. We have not had a white yule in 20 years, and the odds on our warming globe ever offering one must be incalculably long. This isn't Lapland. Christmas snow is but one more EC standard to which we have let ourselves be hijacked. Is it not time to chuck this damaging delusion in?

What it does here at Christmas is rain. We should make this a meterological virtue. Let us have a British Santa in cheery yellow oilskins and sou'wester, ho-ho-ho-ing through the drizzle in a dory tugged by six big cod. Let fake raindrops twinkle down our shop windows from autumn on, let our cards show robins on floating logs and coaches in flying spray, and each display, advertisement and grotto anticipate the joys of snug dry firesides bonding happily families together against the cats and dogs beyond.

Sing *I'm Dreaming of a Wet Christmas*, Cliff, and let's be done with it.

JANUARY

JANUARY

Future Present

I push a button. Oh look, it is New Year's Day 2021! What shall I do? I shall celebrate the centenary of the Naafi. I shall also sow lettuce, radish, and broad beans. I should cut back deciduous shrubs as well, but I am 82, and planting the veg is all my squeaking vertebrae can handle. I shall just hobble back into my house and pour that Naafi stiffie.

I know it is my house, because I have pushed another button and, oh look, I paid off my mortgage on July 21, 1997! The centenary of the Tate Gallery, as a matter of fact: I have made a note of that because there will almost certainly be a big formal knees-up to which they could very well invite me, as a senior hack, and I shouldn't want to miss it. Which I won't, because an alarm will go off, reminding me to get into my tuxedo. I would go there by bus, if I had a bus pass, but, oh look, I have just pushed a button again, and I do not get my bus pass until June 27, 2003, and there's no point going on a bus unless it's free.

And, since you ask, yes, I know exactly what I shall be doing on June 27, 2038. Reading a telegram from the King

133

is what. Unless of course Her Present Majesty is spared, in which case it could well take the gilt off the encandled gingerbread to receive a message from someone of 112, and I a mere ton. Not that I won't have other things on my mind: the car's due for a 400,000-mile service that day. I believe that's one of the major ones, new plugs, new points, everything.

How do I know all this? Can I read the future? Oh yes. No question. I just push buttons, and the future comes up on the screen of my Atari Portfolio personal organizer. Probably, if she's not reading this, the most horrible Christmas present I have ever had. It is an electronic diary which will accept appointments up to and including 2050, when I shall be 112 too, and I have just spent four long days programing it with everything I can think of, all linked to an automatic search and alarm system.

At 128K RAM, the diary claims to be twice the size of its nearest competitor. I would not know about that. I am content to recognize that it is about a million times the size of its nearest owner, a conclusion I came to on Boxing Day when I attempted to enter items which the machine immediately reminded me I had programed in the night before, but had forgotten about. That is part of why I hate it so much: as time goes on, the gap between what it knows about me and what I know about me can only grow wider. When I am finally senile (well before, on present trends, my 112th), it will *be* me. I shall have lost all that I was, and it will have all that there was of me before I lost it.

The rest of what I hate about it is even worse. For one thing, it has forced me to tempt Providence as never before. In order to remind myself to begin collecting my pension, I have to assume I shall be around to collect it. It is an assumption which, I discover, generates a superstitiousness I never knew I possessed. For another thing, in inviting me to jot down the rest of my life, it exposes me to the hitherto carefully repressed recognition that what is guessably to come looks considerably less enjoyable than what has been. Grow old along with me, the second-best is yet to be: *Lose hearing* is not quite so appealing a notional entry as *Lose virginity*.

But most unsettling of all is its peripheral flexibility. This means that the Porfolio may be linked to an external printer, so that every day, from now until 2050, it does not need to have its buttons pressed at all to cough up its contents; it can just wake itself up in the morning with its little buzzer, and print out what I am to do that day. Or, of course, what I would have been doing had I still been around to do it. It is an electronic urn, forever printing and forever young.

"What's that clacketing noise?" they will ask after the funeral. "Oh look, the poor old sod thought he was going to the Thackeray Bicentennial Ball tonight! Life's a funny old game, innit?"

Sex and the Single Vote

I have, I would submit, been a good Eurobrit. The 30 years which spanned the squeak of Ted Heath's nib on the Rome Treaty and last summer's reclassification of the carrot as a fruit never found my compliance wanting. As CAP and Chunnel and EMS, as this standardizing imposition and that, inched slowly towards us – indeed centimetreed slowly towards us – like shy teenage fingers walking the back of a cinema seat towards the finally inescapable embrace, I have neither shrunk away nor slapped the ambitious hand. If Europe was to be turned into the nutritious ecopolitical omelette of the universalist's dream, rich, consistent, without lumps, then nationalist eggs had to be broken, and beaten into milk spilt without tears.

That it might also be a horse designed by a committee was not brought home to me until a few hours ago. A straw was laid across its back. The back broke. Prepared as ever to stand up and be counted, I stood up; but they would not count me.

What has happened is that Miss Tahiti has just become Miss France. She may well go on to become Miss Monde, and if she does, that is exactly what the French will call her, because they have never been slow to nick what suits them, and on this occasion, chauvinism and the Académie Française notwithstanding, they are clearly happy to accept that a Miss is good as a Mlle.

Now, let me quickly say that I have nothing whatever against Miss Tahiti. Not content to be almost two metres of tawny lissomness, topped by a coif of spun gold beneath which a brace of green headlamps burn with a feral intensity which would have had William Blake rethinking the whole principle of matchlessness, Miss Tahiti is also a good egg. She wishes to help world peace and understanding and work among impoverished children, while at the same time becoming an international fashion model, which, you will readily concur, is a hell of a workload: you or I cannot quite see ourselves, can we, mincing down a spotlit catwalk in Mogadishu with a bairn under each arm and a set of unassailable proposals for ending the civil war clenched in our perfect teeth?

My grouse is only that the crown that has been placed upon her lovely head rightfully belongs, in my opinion, upon the marginally lovelier head of Miss Littoral Nord. No, let me be specific: my grouse is that I was not allowed to express that opinion. The French would not let me vote for her.

Now, unlike British television, French television continues to transmit beauty contests in great number. It may be because their feminist lobby is either more or less frivolous than ours, it may simply be that their television is lousier, but whatever the reason, their little screens regularly teem, as ours once did, with young women built mainly of leg, tripping back and forth with that curious rolling hobble which indicates that they are either trying to become Miss Quelquechose or making a final dash for the tape in the 20km walk.

Down here in France to celebrate, with my imminent brethren, the last New Year of our separateness, I switched on the box to find a line of tall girls loping past in identical bathing suits of the kind that allow continuity of thigh and armpit to be interrupted by only the merest thread. Behind them, a winking sign testified that they were going for the Miss France gong, while beneath them flashed the telephone number via which the viewers could vote, for that is how they do things here. The Bastille was not stormed in vain.

Miss Littoral Nord shimmied by. Though shorter than the rest, she displayed that foxy *espièglerie* which has cardinals glumly reviewing their careers. I rang up. Expecting a computer to record my choice I was surprised to find a human monitor interrogating me. My accent is not flawless. Yes, I said, I *am* English, but . . .

The monitor was desolated, but adamant. Not French, I could not vote. I put the phone down, and watched Tahiti come home by a nose. Don't talk to me about Europeanism, and stop dangling that carrot. We both know it's a vegetable.

Needle Match

You have seen *Twelfth Night*, and you therefore know that the whirligig of time brings in his revenges. I say therefore, but you knew it anyway, because you have been through more Twelfth Nights than you care to

137

remember; it is just that Shakespeare put it rather better than you could. He was good at that. He was so good that it is quite possible that when the resonant trope rang across the stalls, you nudged your companion and whispered: "He put his finger right on it, there! That is the top and bottom of Twelfth Night, and no mistake. That is obviously why he called it *Twelfth Night*."

You were close enough. He in fact called it *Twelfth Night* because, then, January 6 was the night when great houses threw great binges wherein the domestic hierarchy was turned topsy-turvy, and through the temporary regency of a Lord of Misrule appointed from among the servants, chaos was allowed free rein. The fun started with everyone running around disguised as everyone else and sloshing one another with pig's bladders, from which things went from bad to the point where they cannot be reported in a modern newspaper, lest the butler happen to spot them while ironing it and get ideas likely to cause a breach of the peace. For the present age is sexually less flexible than Shakespeare's and may start asking awkward questions when familiar lipstick turns up on the footman's doublet and people come down to breakfast in odd socks. Which is why – not wishing to turn our backs totally upon the tradition – we have substituted an inanimate object for the Lord of Misrule, thereby lowering the moral risks, but losing none of the chaos.

The inanimate object is called a Christmas tree; it mounts the whirligig of time on Christmas Eve, and when the whirligig brings it round to January 6, it exacts its revenge. It runs from servant to master, it takes over the great house, and, by nightfall, it sees to it that those whom it has loyally and meekly served for 12 jolly days shall be left in gibbering, anaphylactic shock.

Mind you, to be fairer to ours than I should currently prefer, it did give early warning of its vindictive streak. Readers who had nothing better to do on page 124 than push on to page 126 may recall my telling them how the 10ft thing had burst its bonds on the car trip home, and was retrussed with police string after they had stopped what appeared to be a Norwegian fir galloping through Hampstead with a man in it. It could be retrussed, then, because it was springy, it could be carried indoors because the binding made it 3ft in diameter. Unbound, it was 8ft, and when, having left it for a week, we returned from France on Sunday, we found that rigor mortis had set in and it could not be retrussed at all. Not only skeletal and waist-deep in its own brown detritus, it was stiff as a brick. We do not have 8ft doorways. It would have to be sawn up.

Misrule began. As in a horror film, the corpse retained some manic and malicious vitality; when, impatient as any murderer, I tugged at its jewellery – its lights, its baubles, its tinsel, its little Santas and fairies – it twitched and fell, measuring its length in the hall, spilling a hundredweight of earth from its tub, and swiping two pictures from the wall. Forensic scientists would make a meal of this, I thought, even as I took the hacksaw to its supine limbs. A horrible business: we had sung and drunk beside it, we had exchanged gifts and greetings of goodwill, we had crept past it to soft beds while it continued selflessly to twinkle through its working nights, exuding pine and cheer, and now I was sawing its arms off. Do murderers feel such pangs? Is the revenge of corpses always so complex?

It would not be disposed of. It would not burn on the bonfire, only smoulder. I wondered what that smell was, said my neighbour, two eyes above the dark fence. I felt the ozone layer flinch. I went back into the hall to shovel earth. That rug's had it, said my wife.

On Monday, the picture-framer said: say sixty quid, plus VAT. The man in the Hoover shop said what is it, needles in the works again?

Take Down This Book

When I tell them that I was on my way to the Garrick Club last Tuesday, regular readers will understand why my little heart was going pit-a-pat. They will remember that the last time I went to the Garrick, some ratbag stole my new blue overcoat from what they call the gentleman's cloakroom, for all the world as if it were a cloakroom patronized by gentlemen. And since that overcoat has never reappeared – except, of course, in South America, as part of the regular consignment of swag filched from visiting non-members and shipped aboard the rusty scow which the Garrick brigandage keeps conveniently moored at Westminster pier with its engine running – you will, I know, sympathize with the palpitations rhythmically buckling the upper slopes of the new brown overcoat which replaced it.

For the new brown overcoat had never been to the Garrick before, and this could thus be its last sight of England, despite the fact that Mummy had been up all night sewing name-tapes into not only it, but also my brown felt hat and my umbrella: because, given the sleet, I needed all three, notwithstanding the risks attendant on the huge amounts they could command upon the streets of Buenos Aires, where anything with a Swaine, Adeney & Brigg label is quoted, such is the meld of Latin chic and Latin inflation, not in pesos but in eye-teeth.

Now, in order to carry victims from Cricklewood to the Garrick, the No 13 bus is required to pause in its Regent

Street trundle and heave to outside the Café Royal, doubt-less to enable lucky peripolitan rednecks to catch a glimpse of famous corporate lunchers following their Havanas through the swing-doors. But as I glanced down from the upper deck in the hope of being able to tell my future grand-children that I had once seen the Chief Executive of Wunda-trash Toilet Novelties plc, a yet more memorable sight interrupted the dropping eye. On the roof of the bus-stop's shelter, its sodden pages flicking in the gale, lay a book. And not just any old book, either; being a mere 5ft above it, I could see at once that it was *The Oxford Dictionary of Quotations*, that distillation of the precious life-blood of a thousand master spirits without which the simple hack would have to find a less felicitous way of describing it.

The brain thrummed in counterpoint to the 13's idling crankshaft: what kind of person defenestrates an *ODQ* from the Café Royal? A literary diner, forearmed to crush a dila-tory waiter with a witheringly apt quote, but unable to find it? A volatile bimbette who had bought it in Hatchards as a present for a chief executive who had promised to tell his wife all, but who, over the quail, had explained that, sorry, his wife hadn't been feeling very well lately? A drunken member of the Wisley Rugby Club in a private suite reunion, reminding them of how he had settled the 1973 Hornchurch match with a drop goal in the final seconds?

I looked at my watch. Ten full minutes remained to my appointment. I clattered down the stairs, ran into the Café Royal and up to the reception desk. "Should one of your guests ask you if anybody's handed in a copy of *The Oxford Dictionary of Quotations*," I said, "you might tell him it's on top of the bus-shelter outside."

The chap stared at me with the eyes of someone who is suddenly looking forward to getting home so that his wife can ask him what kind of a day he's had, but all he said was: "Thank you, sir."

I got to the Garrick bang on time, puffed but smug, met my host, and went to hang up my hat and coat in as secure a spot as possible. It was as I was wondering whether to ask the porter for a padlock that it was borne in on me that I was not hanging up my umbrella. This was because I did not have my umbrella. The 13 bus had my umbrella.

"Ah," said my host, after I had cursed for a bit, "we are to dumb Forgetfulness a prey." I didn't think he had the quotation quite right, but since the only way to check was to run back to Regent Street and shin up the bus-shelter, I said nothing.

And anyway, it was one fewer item for the Garrick to nick.

The Day War Broke Out

I really must ring Dame Vera Lynn. She is the expert. I want to ask her when Johnny can sleep in his own little room again.

Indeed, I was rather surprised not to have heard her interviewed on that subject last night; or, as it seamlessly became, this morning. Every other military expert was being grilled, including a venerable cove who had covered the relief of Mafeking for the *Morning Post*, unless I am very much mistaken, which I could well have been, given that an egg had just fallen on my foot, and those of you who know that an egg on a kitchen floor at 5am is able to cover an area 12 feet square will sympathize, I know, with someone struggling to get albumen off the sole of his slipper while trying to follow events in the Gulf. The *Morning Post* bloke was being invited by GLR or LBC or some such to offer a snap judgment on the efficacy of laser-directed artillery in adverse weather conditions, but from his prevaricative answer and the elderly quaver in the voice delivering it, it seemed to me that he still had an open mind on whether the arquebus would replace the halberd.

That is the misfortune of minor radio in times like these: the top pundits having all been retained to shout the odds on major outlets, Radio Cricklewood can count itself lucky if it can find the telephone number of a former Home Guard corporal prepared to offer his expert view of what, exactly, would be going through Saddam Hussein's mind at, er, this moment in time.

Of course, Dame Vera might well have been on, only I missed her: apart from my somewhat frenetic channel-hopping (which could have meant that while I was tuned to Radio 4 and listening to three Americans standing on their Baghdad lavatory seat for a better view of what had just gone bang, Dame Vera was singing her heart out on BSkyB and showing us a Woolton Pie she had prepared earlier) I also had the kipper out of the window for a good five minutes, during which time I couldn't hear anything.

Graham Gooch has much to answer for. Had Gooch been fit, I should have been a far more efficient noctambulist. As early as last October, when January 15 was nothing more than a gleam on George Bush's personal organizer, I was girding the loin for midnight confrontation and its accompanying vigil (even now, I half expect to switch on and hear John Simpson telling me that the desert will almost certainly begin to take spin on the fourth day). Prepared to change both my timetable and my metabolism to follow the Ashes commentary through the night, I ensured that the fridge was well-stocked with the sort of stuff you need at 2am, when the bails come off for lunch and the listening juices spurt in concert.

But it all went wrong. Gooch took a smack on the digit, whereafter things rapidly accelerated from bad to unthinkable, and injury after injury brought the inevitable addition of insult after insult. What point was there in staying up all night, just to hear the snick of English outside edges? By

Christmas, I had put myself back on a daytime footing, which meant that when war came, it found me both untrained and unprepared. Nevertheless gentlemen in England could not remain a-bed: at midnight on the 16th, I left my own little room, padded down to the kitchen, switched on the radio and turned the dial to Armageddon.

You know the rest. A listener marches on his stomach. At 5am, notwithstanding the general momentousness, I felt in need of a little something; but the little something put by to accompany flannelled folly had long ago been eaten. I opened the fridge; there was an egg in the fridge; and soon after that, because my untrained fingers had been up all night, there was an egg on the floor.

Which is why I came to be holding a kipper out of the window. For there is nothing likelier to irritate a household than waking to the reek of lingering kipper-fumes, and the only way I know of mitigating this is to white-heat the pan, chuck in the fish, and hold both out of the kitchen window until one has fried the other.

Who could have guessed, last August, what psychic ravages the Iraqi invasion of Kuwait would one day wreak on next door's cat? It was through its flap like a ginger Exocet, pacing the party fence and howling for kipper like a thing possessed. Today, it will be in even worse shape than I am. How long must this go on? What will it take to get Dame Vera into a radio car?

Cakes and Ale

My tuxedo is a broken reed this morning. Anyone can see that. Its zest is gone, its mohair nap is flat; its silk lapels have lost their healthy gloss; its buttons hang listless from their threads, like the eyes of clapped-out teddies. Were it a dog, I should have to scoop it up and rush it down to the vet's for a prod and a powder.

What has brought this on is fathomless disappointment. The tuxedo thought it was going walkies. Not to say dancies. For more than a month now, sleeve and trouser alike had dreamed of porting svelte cosmopolites backwards through as chic a throng as ever foxtrotted a welcome to the rising dawn, a rumba here, a samba there, pausing between rounds only to pop a crab claw down and sluice its passage with Dom Perignon. For the event to which the tuxedo had been invited, so the gossip columns clarioned, was to have been the knees-up of the year, where its shoulders would have rubbed those belonging to 500 of the rich, the famous, the powerful, the beautiful, the royal. Is it then any wonder that, today, they droop so glumly from their hanger?

Because today, the tuxedo received a letter. "Sadly," it was told, "in view of the current Gulf crisis, we have decided to postpone the party we had scheduled for Tuesday, February 12, 1991. At such a grim time in the world, none of us feels a party would be appropriate."

Had the tuxedo nerveless fingers, this letter would have dropped from them. But since it did not have fingers at all, the letter had to be read aloud to it, and the person reading it was thus in a perfect position to observe the tuxedo's first reaction. This was not disappointment – that came later, when the truth sank in – but disbelief. Surely, it was for just such moments as these that it had been tailored? Cometh the hour, cometh the suit?

Now, before you rush to outraged judgment on the tuxedo's insensitivity, pointing out that millions of decent people in this great country of ours are being forced, in these dark days, to sacrifice far more – such as having *'Allo, 'Allo* pulled – and asking where a suit gets off complaining about losing nothing more than a night on the tiles, perhaps I should explain that the tuxedo did not come to this conclusion alone. It was heavily influenced by the suit which, for many years now, has hung beside it. This, too, is a tuxedo (though it prefers to be called a dinner-jacket) but of a far older cut and weight; a roomy double-breasted number, hewn from heavy black barathea, it belonged to the father of the tuxedo's owner, and now hangs in the offspring's wardrobe as the result of Time's behaving like an ever-rolling stream.

It is a pretty old suit. It was made for the father's 1935 marriage. But that was not its best time: its best time came five years later, when it suddenly started to go out and enjoy itself a hell of a lot. Its owner would come home on leave, climb out of his uniform and into his dinner-jacket, and take his wife to all manner of places, like Ciro's and the Trocadero and the Savoy and the Ace of Spades, where the suit would hurtle about to the strict tempi of Bert Ambrose and Roy Fox and Geraldo and Jack Payne and Snakehips Johnson, despite the fact that the night sky above these venues was regularly criss-crossed with searchlights, that the saxophones were periodically drowned by a more insistent wail, and that occasionally, when the suit was making its way home, it would notice that some of the buildings which had been there on its way in were there no longer.

And being an old suit, it will, naturally, not be slow to reminisce. Though the wardrobe's owner cannot be sure of the exact words, since his command of Suit is as inadequate as the next man's, his conviction is unshaken that the old dinner-jacket will be much given to evoking the the spirit of the Blitz, when the cry was business as usual, and when, in bomb-shelter and nightspot alike, Mother Brown's knees were always up and *Run, Adolf, Run* was the chart-topper, because it was all a matter of *nil carborundum*, and the last thing any Briton would dream of doing was letting some tinpot bloody dictator think he was having any effect at all.

When, in short, anyone writing "At such a grim time in the world, none of us feels a party would be appropriate," ran the grave risk of instantly being identified as a fifth-columnist, and hanged from the nearest turned-round signpost.

FEBRUARY

Same Old Game

Today is a very good day for me. It is also a very good day for partridge and pheasant, though they won't know that until tomorrow, which will be an even better day. For snipe, woodcock and capercaillie, of course, today is the even better day, since today is the tomorrow it was yesterday, which was still only a very good day, although naturally they didn't know it, then.

Because it is only human beings who know that February 1 is the last day of the shooting season. Partridge and pheasant have no idea. Tell them the date is February 1, and they will look at you blankly, imagining it to be a day like any other. They will get up, they will peck at the ostensibly generous breakfast which has been chucked out for them every morning these four months past to ensure that they grow large enough to hit, and after they have been pecking for a while, people will start making a lot of noise behind them, banging sticks on trees and rattling rattles, and the pheasants and the partridge will attempt to get away from this for a bit of peace and quiet, only to discover that what they have got away to is a bit of war and noise. Since many of them will then fall down with holes in, never mind ending

151

up in a dog's mouth, you can see why even those who survive will not twig that it is a very good day. They will not twig this until tomorrow, when they will get up and peck and wait to be driven out and shot at, only it will not happen, because it will be February 2.

I suppose it's just possible that one or two of the older hands – wings, rather – might have, today, an inkling of the imminent Armistice, provided there is a woodcock or a capercaillie around, or even, if the terrain is propitious, a snipe.

That is because older pheasant or partridge, who have survived earlier seasons, may recognize in the smug strut of the now-unassailable woodcock its awareness that it is not being shot at, and remember what happened last year, i.e., the day after people stopped shooting at woodcock, they stopped shooting at pheasant and partridge. Quite why it should be that the open season for woodcock, capercaillie and snipe should end at midnight on January 31, but for pheasant and partridge it should end 24 hours later, I do not know, unless it is that the former have a smarter lawyer.

What I do know is that the end of the shooting season is almost as good a day for me as it is for the birds. They can stop dying, which means that I can stop eating them. This will be a great relief. I have eaten large numbers of them during the past four months, and I have not enjoyed a single one. That this has anything to do with animal politics may be quickly scotched (like the only woodcock I do enjoy) and dispatched as the foul canard it is (and not only because within that phrase lurk two even worse jokes than the wood-cock one), for I have nothing against the shooting of birds. I enjoy eating strangled ones, and since, if you are a bird, copping it on the wing after an even-money dash for freedom must be preferable to gargling your last beneath the slaughterer's inescapable thumb, the eater of roast chicken cannot point the greasy finger at the shooter of roast pheasant.

My complaint is simply that I prefer that chicken (and that goose, and that turkey, and that unwild duck) to riddled game on a number of counts, the prime of which leads the rest by a furlong. For though I also prefer the flavour, the texture, and the unrun risk to expensive bridgework from a mouthful of pellets, far more than any of these I prefer the absence of anecdote.

Over the past few years, shooting has become maniacally popular among the middle-aged townies who constitute my circle. I never see them at winter weekends any more, because they are all out shooting. I see them only during the evenings, when I have not only to eat what they have shot but to hear how they shot it, and where, and what they shot it with, and the cost of shooting it. I listen to all this politely, cautiously chewing my gutta-percha gobbet, spitting shot into the receptacle provided, nodding and smiling uncomprehendingly at each arcane detail, and attempting to look as though I am getting full value from the hundred-quid wreckage in front of me.

But secretly wondering if Colonel Sanders has a branch on my way home. I like dining with him. Not only do you not break teeth, he doesn't sit down beside you and explain how he strangled your dinner.

Doom'd For a Certain Term to
Walk the Night

The woman at the all-night unisex sauna in East Finchley was really very nice. Heart of gold. "Yes," she said, "there *used* to be an all-night chemist in this parade, but it shuts at nine o'clock now."

153

I liked "parade". I hadn't heard the word in a long time. It took me back. There were a lot of parades about when I was young. There were also a lot of all-night chemists.

"Sorry to barge in on you," I said, "it's just that your light was on. I drove down here because Golders Green police station said they thought there was an all-night chemist, but I couldn't see anywhere else open."

"There's only us and the Iranian grocer," said the sauneuse. "Funny they didn't direct you to Warman-Freed in Golders Green Road. I think they're open all night. Shall I look up their number?"

"That's all right, thanks," I said, "I know where you mean."

It was 2am when I got to Warman-Freed. It was closed.

"Shuts at midnight," said the man in the all-night pizza parlour opposite. He was very nice, too. He turned from the coffee machine and said, loudly: "Anyone knows where there's an all-night chemist?"

The half-dozen customers glanced up from their iridescent wedges. Five shook their heads, but a man in a herringbone overcoat said: "You want bliss."

Who, I thought, doesn't? Since, however, I also wanted the bottle of Distalgesic and the course of Amoxyl for which their prescription and I had been trawling the streets since half-past twelve, I took the chance that the herringbone overcoat housed more than a peckish evangelist doom'd for a certain term to walk the night, and repeated: "Bliss?"

"All-night chemist, corner of Walm Lane and Kilburn High Road."

I stood looking at the dark windows of Bliss for a bit, until the man from the all-night minicabbery across the road strolled over and said, "All night? *All night?* They haven't been open all night for what, got to be three years, could be four, we've been here, what . . . ?"

So I asked him, because it was the sort of thing a minicabbie ought to know, and he said: "No problem, John Bell & Croyden, get anything there, any time, Wigmore Street, on the left, just past that wossname, that all-night video place, what's it called, it'll come to me in a minute . . ."

It took me twenty, and I came to it because when I came to John Bell & Croyden, though the outside lamplight winked cheerily off scalpel sets and sphygmomanometers and stethoscopes and curious prostheses and tiny aluminium baths for this unfathomable purpose and that, no light at all shone from within.

"You're going back a bit," said the proprietor of 24-Hour Video Rental. "They stopped their all-night service donkey's years ago."

"Only place I know," said a customer, piling four dubious cassettes beside the till, "is Boots at Piccadilly Circus."

"He probably meant Boots at Marble Arch," said the man behind the till at the all-night souvenir shop opposite Boots at Piccadilly Circus, where two young Japanese were trying on policemen's helmets, but if he did, he was wrong there, too, as anyone who has stood outside the Boots at Marble Arch at 3.30am will tell you.

So I went into an all-night coffee shop at the top of Edgware Road, and I had a large espresso, and I asked them if I could use their phone, and I rang the Royal Free Hospital because it was on what was going to be my way home, now, and I told them about how I had this prescription for my daughter who had this extremely painful ear infection, and could they possibly supply the medication, and they said not unless I brought the ear in and they diagnosed it first, and I said that was impossible but was there an all-night chemists anywhere between Land's End and John O'Groats, and they said not that they knew of.

So I came home, and my wife said it was okay. Victoria was asleep now and it could wait till morning, and I pointed out that it *was* bloody morning, and I was going upstairs to write this piece about the greatest metropolis in the world and how you could get everything you wanted any hour of the day or night, saunas, pizzas, videos, minicabs, policemen's helmets, you name it – remember how it was when you were a kid, you couldn't get anything after midnight, except medicine.

155

Bottling Out

I t is September 1940, and a man is standing on the very
cusp of post-lapsarian France. Indeed, it is possible that
his left foot stands on the occupied north, his right on the
Vichy south, but what he is standing on is not as important as
what he is standing in. Because we are at Pauillac, just north
of Bordeaux and both the epicentre and apogee (if the purer
geometricians among you will grant me that licence) of the
trade to which the city gives its name. It will not, therefore,
surprise you to hear that the man is standing in a vat. For
the 1940 *vendange* has just been gathered, and he is poised
to jump about on it.

It has been a funny old year for him. When the plump
items beneath his toes were naught but a pip in their fathers'
eye, the first of that sequence of events was precipitated
which was so rapidly to bring Rommel and Guderian and all
their jolly *Kameradschaft* blitzing down the road towards
him, casting (for he is a practical fellow) grave doubts on the
imminent vintage: since, when it comes to pressing grapes,
nothing can hold a candle to a Tiger tank.

He need not have worried; connoisseurs all, the German
high command was never going to shell claret. They were
not going to churn up Lafite, nor have their Stukas dive onto
Margaux, for there is no point whatever in occupying France
if there's nothing to drink but parachuted Riesling. That is
why they hit the brakes just outside Pauillac on that June

156

afternoon, and sensibly waited for Pétain to chuck in the towel.

Let us now leave our hero there, with his trousers rolled up, and move the scene half a century forward to January 1991 and the basement of Selfridges. For it is here that Sears plc is holding a charity auction of rare wines, to which they have invited, among others, a fool and his money. Much comes and goes under the gavel, wondrous '61s and '66s and '70s, calculated to so slip down a treat that choking on the price would instantly be forgotten, but the fool does not bid for any of these. He is waiting for a bottle of Château Duhart-Milon to come up, a fourth-growth Pauillac of which he knows nothing except that its label bears the date 1940. The fool has never drunk a 1940 claret, and when the moment comes, he bids with such sociopathic ferocity that under-bidders end up counting themselves fortunate not to have been bigger fools than he is, for it is a long way home in the dark, if you are carrying a bottle of which you have deprived a madman.

Not that your homeward worries are any the less if you are the madman. You begin to wonder how you will ever get around to drinking something this rare, not to say this expensive. Old wines are not like other antiques: you do not bring home a T'ang horse and hit it with a hammer, you do not run back from Sothebys with a Chippendale chair and immediately bung it on the fire, but you cannot enjoy an antique wine unless you destroy it. And how, precisely, will you go about destroying it? What meal could match it? Which of your friends will you invite to share it, which will you offend by not inviting?

But most to the point, what do you do when you get it home, rush to your wine-books, and discover that the authorities speak with one voice on the 1940 vintage, which is that "wartime circumstances made it untrustworthy"? Well, if you have the presumption, you ring Jancis Robinson in the hope that she will say it is not untrustworthy at all, but Jancis too says it could be great, it could be terrible; either way, drink it quickly after you've opened it, because it could die within a few minutes, and you ring off, and you look at it. Not going to be much of an evening, ask three friends over for five minutes, pull the cork, get that down you, what do you think, great, terrible, good-night.

Which is why a month has now passed, with the cork still in. During which time I have given more thought to the untrustworthiness of the 1940 vintage. Might it possibly depend on whether the bloke standing in the Duhart-Milon vat was a patriot or a collaborator? If you thought that what you were about to tread was going to end up lubricating the Nazi gullet, would you try to ensure that it was as delicious as possible, or would you, how shall I put it, take advantage of the fact that you were about to be waist-deep in what the bastard wouldn't see until his batman sloshed it into the regimental crystal?

Table Flap

It was a crazy time to open a restaurant. Nobody's eating out, except journalists charged with writing articles on why nobody's eating out.

But a restaurateur's got to dream, boy: it comes with the territory.

Especially when the territory looks the way it does at the moment, and when the restaurateur has had the dream for 40 years, ever since he sat in scripture classes doodling moustaches on seraphim, filling in the "o"s in The Book of Revelations, redrawing the endpaper map of the Holy Land to include Piglet's house, but scrupulously (some might say religiously) leaving unvandalized the colour plate with the dream in it.

It showed a little *al fresco* place in Assisi. The owner was sitting at its one table, with a rabbit in front of him. He was not eating the rabbit. It was the rabbit who was eating. The rabbit was a customer. Beside it, a chicken family was tucking in, and down the further end of the table, a couple of tortoises were sharing a side-salad. The place was obviously doing fantastic business: not only was a mouse taking lunch in the owner's hand, and a party of wrens pecking seed off his knee, but a large blue bird was standing on one of his shoulders, and a ginger cat was curled up on the other; clearly, they had failed to book, but were prepared to wait.

I cannot now recall what the homiletic subtext of all this was supposed to be, I know only that the overt message was plain: if the joint was clean, the food good, the patron jolly, and the prices reasonable, animals would beat a path to your door. I never forgot this, even though it took me a long time to get around to acting upon it.

Last Sunday, I opened my first restaurant.

Early that morning, a man on the radio said that wildlife was under threat from the snow. Birds in particular could not get enough to eat. He then gave a long list of what birds liked.

It was amazing. You did not need worms and ants to open a restaurant, nor berries and seeds; the modern bird was patently as prone to gourmet faddery as the rest of us. What it was into these days was wholemeal bread, muesli, bacon rind, crushed walnuts, grated cheese, cornflakes . . .

I hinged upright in bed. I had all that stuff. I could clean up. I could be Francis Roux, the ornithoculinary brother, three Michelin beaks, the Birdman of Cricklewood. All I did not have was the premises. I should have to erect a birdtable. I wellied up, and went into the garden. But the lawn beneath the snow was granite, there was no question of banging in a post and nailing a platform to it – and then I remembered the cocktail trolley. A gift so naff it had never left the garage, it would unquestionably, now, be just the

159

thing: you have to have a gimmick in the restaurant game, and could I not hear one bird telling another how it had eaten in this really wacky place, it had two big wheels and two little wheels, and titchy individual cubicles set into the floor. The Muesli Room, The Rindery, The Cheese 'n' Walnut Suite . . .

I hurried back inside, and into the kitchen, whereupon I discovered that the stuff I'd thought I had was not quite as I'd imagined: the bacon had no rind, the cheese was soft and grater-resistant, the walnuts were pecans, the cornflakes were Coco Pops, and so on – yet, on reflection, might these too, not constitute a marketing plus, sweeping the smart winged world with their chic novelty? There was, after all, a time when people thought kiwi was boot-polish, gave monkfish to the cat, and, when offered a board of goat-cheeses, politely asked the waiter when the man was coming to do the drains.

So I sliced the bacon into delicate strips, chopped the Camembert into tiny cubes, crushed the pecans into beak-sized morsels, and I decanted them into separate compartments in the trolley alongside the Coco Pops and the chunks of granary bread, and I went back into the house, and I took covert station at an upstairs window, as any eager new restaurateur would, and I sat there for an hour and no-one came, and I kept going back for the next six hours, and no-one came, and at four o'clock it started to snow again, and by half-past, the entire untouched *smorgasbord* was covered, as if it had never been.

I tell you, nobody's eating out these days. Ask any journalist.

Pussy Galore

None of this would be a problem if the cat didn't have a cerebrum. Because it has a cerebrum, it is capable of rational thought, and because it is capable of rational thought, it may well have a reason for doing what it does. I need to discover what it is.

Until yesterday morning, I knew neither that cats had cerebra, nor that they could mull things over with them. Cats' brains were a closed book to me, before I opened *The Concise Encyclopaedia of Cats*. I found it in Child's Hill Public Library, while the cat waited outside. When I came out again, the cat looked up at me, so I showed it the book, because, by dint of a cursory flip while the librarian did her stuff, I had by that time discovered that it had a cerebrum, and I wanted to keep it abreast of developments. Then I walked home. The cat followed. It's about a mile.

"Do you have a lot of cats?" the librarian had enquired, stamping.

"None," I replied. "But one's been following me for three days. I thought I'd try to find out why."

"It loves you," said the librarian. "They do that, with catpeople."

"I am not a catperson," I said.

The librarian smiled a catperson's smile. "You may not *think* you are," she said.

The cat had picked me up on Monday morning. I was taking my usual short-cut home through Hampstead

161

Cemetery, and I had paused at the mottled headstone of Vitruvius Wyatt (1824–1897) to wonder why anyone should be christened Vitruvius, when the cat came out from behind it. It was a predominantly black cat, but with a half-white face – as if Andrew Lloyd Webber, having wisely concluded that his musical bucket could not go twice to the well, had decided to tailor his ambitions to *The Cat of the Opera* – and a white tail.

I paid it no attention, and strolled on. It strolled after. When I stopped at the tomb of James Clarke, landlord of Jack Straw's Castle, to regret that nobody in 1913 had mustered the facetiousness to chisel *Time, Please!* above his remains, the cat stopped, too. And when I hurried on (for graveyards have a way of suddenly reminding you not to hang about) the cat likewise put boot to throttle. I arrived home, and it stopped at the step; I opened the front door, but it showed no inclination to enter. It was not after food or shelter. What was it after?

It sat there all day, but whether it vanished with the gloaming or merely because of it, I did not notice. Certainly, it had gone by midnight, when I put out the empty milk bottles; but when I took in the full ones on Tuesday morning, it was back. It did not stir until noon, when I walked a mile to the shops. It sat outside three of them, then it walked back at my heels. I stopped at West Hampstead nick, and went in to ask if anyone had reported a lost cat, but they said they didn't do cats, it's bad enough doing dogs, try sticking a note on the gate, so I came out again, and the cat got off the bonnet of a Panda and fell back in step. It spent the afternoon outside my front door again, was gone at midnight, and back on Wednesday morning. We walked to the library.

The encyclopaedia was not the only book we borrowed. We also took out Desmond Morris's *Catwatching* and, God help us, Beverley Nichols's *Cats A–Z*. Useless, the pair of them: Mr Morris has 60 chapter with titles like *Why do Cats Eat Grass?* and *Why does a Cat Wag its Tail?* but you will search in vain for *Why does a Cat Follow You up the Pub?* and Beverley Nichols says F stands for fur. Since he also

162

says the best way to appreciate a cat's fur is to have a candle-lit dinner with it, I saw little point in investigating what he had entered under P. The odds against Beverley and his moggie ever having tied a few on at the Cricklewood Tavern seemed somewhat long.

It is Thursday morning as I write, the cat is back on the front step, and I do not know what to do next. I had planned to take a walk across Hampstead Heath, but as it is generally full of tattooed blokes with alsatians and rottweilers at their heels, I should feel a bit of a . . .

A bit of a catperson.

Bear Bait

I was in Leeds on Tuesday, handing a chicken leg to a grizzly bear, when a thought struck me. It was not unconnected with the fact that, somewhere above my head, Yorkshire Television Holdings had just coughed up £5.1 million for a 19.07 per cent stake in Tyne Tees Television; for market analysts had concluded from this first foray that YTV might some day take over TTTV in the hope of controlling the fireside entertainment of the entire North East, and should that happen, it would have a direct bearing on the careers of both me and the bear.

The bear and I had convened for the purpose of recording a further shimmering half hour of YTV's *Through the Keyhole*, that splendid divertissement which not only launched the unique vowels of Mr Loyd Grossman upon a baffled world, but also – as if this were not enough – granted the rich

163

and famous the opportunity of inviting ten million weekly snoopers onto their premises to see what they have in the fridge. Best of all, though, it provides work for moonlighting hacks who might otherwise have nothing to do after moonrise, since the show requires more than just Mr Grossman, more even than Mr David Frost, flower of quiz-hosts, and more yet than an unending gallimaufry of incautious celebrities eager to expose their boudoirs to ridicule. It also requires a three-man panel whose job it is to stare at a clip of film and attempt to guess whose keyhole the camera has gone through. The homeowner is then fanfared in as a guest – or, more typically, unguessed – to be presented by David with a priceless goldette key.

I have been a member of that panel for five proud years, and it was therefore more than my usual trepidation which convulsed me when I found, on Tuesday, the studios shrill with such rumours as mergers always generate, for the one thing worse than stage-fright is non-stage fright, i.e., the terror that someone is going to take your stage away. If YTV and TTTV welded themselves into YTTTV, would *Through the Keyhole* survive? You dared not ask. You merely strode manfully into make-up to let someone put a brave face on you, and you went out there to do your thing.

The recording began as unabnormally as ever, the host bounced on, the audience cheered, the lights went down, and upon the giant studio monitor the mystery house materialized, with the irrepressible Loyd shimmying through it, dropping such clues as his mangling glottis permitted us to decode. They were not enough: we hummed, we hawed, but we chucked in, finally, the sponge. At this, more than his customary glee suffused old Frosty's face; he pivoted towards the audience and asked them if they would welcome, please – Hercules the Bear!

Hercules came on. Hercules filled the set. Hercules was a ginger mountain. He had with him a trainer, but when you saw the two of them together, the word seemed nominal. If the caprice took Hercules, you felt, the trainer might be called lunch. Indeed, Hercules *was* hungry: the trainer kept giving him chicken legs. Hercules ate them while he looked at you. Little could be more unsettling; you felt that all that stood between you and Hercules was *hors-d'oeuvres*. Then Hercules put his head on my desk. He has the world's biggest head. The desk sagged. The trainer handed me a chicken leg. Hercules looked at it.

This was when the thought struck me. I know what is happening, I thought. A decision has indeed been taken upstairs. But they are not going to take *Through the Keyhole* off, they are going to have it eaten. It is cheaper than writing contracted people out of the series, it invites far less tabloid hassle about changing corporate policies, it requires no fraught explanations to the ITC, it is environment-friendly, ideologically sound on animal rights, and will bring only sympathetic publicity to YTV – *Entire Cast of Popular Game Show Eaten by Bear: A Nation Mourns*. I held out the leg and waited for Hercules to carry on up the arm. I am an old trouper. *It was the way he would have wanted to go, weeps widow.*

But Hercules turned away. He looked at his trainer. His trainer looked at me. A long hush fell. You could feel *Through the Keyhole* hanging in the balance.

"It's your cufflinks," said the trainer, finally. "They've put him off."

I have saved the show. Thank you, shirt. Thank me, world.

MARCH

Dish of the Day

et me quickly say that I have nothing against immortality. And let me almost as quickly say that the immortality I have nothing against is, of course, the metaphorical variety, because, even if it existed, I should have a great deal against the other sort. It would be no fun at all waking up on your billionth birthday, opening your billionth batch of jocular cards, and trying to think of somewhere different to go for dinner.

No, the immortality under inspection here is the only one currently on offer to us, *viz* the immortality that might come your way after your mortality had run its inevitable course – what should, I suppose, more properly be called paramortality. It is little more, really, than the property of being remembered; for though we are all footprints in the sands of time, if we may so arrange it that a little fortifying cement is sprinkled in that mortal wake to enable posterity to stand on the crest of time's windy dune, point to the indentation and say "Oh look, old so-and-so passed this way!", we shall be the happier to pop our clogs, knowing that our libbin' has not been in vain.

Especially if we had helped somebody as we rolled along. Because that little more than the property of being remembered is the being remembered benevolently, something yet harder to ensure. If we are one of the rare ones, of course, we can jot down *King Lear*, or spot the Awayday potential of a rattling kettle-lid, or come up with a recipe for stout, but if we belong to the vast majority of common ones, then there is generally not a great deal we can do to guarantee that, after the earth has rattled on our own lid, our name will be legion and our works extolled. Oh, we can plant a magnolia, or make a video of our weekend in Rhyl, or have our A-level certificate tastefully framed for subsequent bequest, but as hedges against perishability, these cannot be said to count for much.

They know this at Heritage Ceramics Inc., Denver, Col. I know that they know this because they have written to tell me so. It may well be that they have also written to you, because there is nothing special about me; I know that there is nothing special about me because, if there were, Heritage Ceramics wouldn't have written to me. They wouldn't have offered me An Invitation to Become Your Own Heirloom.

Here is how it works. You send Heritage Ceramics two personal items: one is a photograph with your face on it, the other is a cheque with your signature on it. Having put the latter in their out-tray, they take your photograph from their in-tray, and they pass it to master-ceramicists working in the time-honoured traditions of their craft. These worthy fellows transfer-print your face, and glaze it in kilns, not once but four times, ensuring that it is proofed to a resistance twice as high as that which attaches to the toughest dishwasher. They do this because you are now a 106-piece dinner-service. Your face is grinning up not merely from plates and bowls, but also from oven-to-table tureens and serving-ladles. It need not be your face alone, either: you may wish to be a husband-and-wife dinner service, but since this is mentioned only in a footnote, I conclude that Heritage Ceramics have looked at the divorce statistics and concluded that deathless crockery might have its embarrassments, too.

170

They prefer to emphasize the boons: "Just think, two centuries from now, your ancestors could be sitting down to a formal dinner off . . ." I pause, because while they cry "– off this unique family heirloom", I think "– off your face". It is 2191, and I am gazing up at my descendants through a puddle of consommé. The next course comes, and now I lie hidden beneath gammon and two veg, to be gradually revealed as an ancestor with a pea in one eye, a carrot where his nose should be, and a shard of gristle in his hair.

Now it is pudding time, and I am being hurried from oven-to-table, and, oh look, my contents have boiled over, I am just a chin emerging from beneath a treacle caul. "Who's that?" shriek the children. "Why," replies their mother, "it is Great-great-great-great Grandpa Coren, of course, and take that smirk off your faces, he is worth a fortune, despite the crack in his ladle . . ."

I do believe I'll take a raincheck, Heritage. No offence, but I know where I can lay my hands on a really sturdy magnolia.

The Cricklewood House

L e Carré is right. He is not just whistling to keep our spirits down. The structure is still in place. Nothing has changed.

It did not start like Le Carré, mind. It started like Graham Greene. Le Carré would not dream of kicking off with the doormatting of a crumpled scrap of paper in an unattributable envelope, because melodrama has no place in espionage. Which shows you that though he may be right about some things, he is wrong about Cricklewood.

Do not blame him. Cricklewood is a riddle wrapped in a mystery inside an enigma. Even I did not know about The Russian Centre. Until, that is, the unidentified correspondent posted me, last Tuesday, the crumpled scrap of paper. Uncrumpled it read: "CERAMICS FROM RUSSIA IN CRICKLEWOOD: The Russian Centre, 303 Cricklewood Broadway NW2."

It was torn from a spiski.

I do not know what a spiski is. I know only that the single paragraph ran: "The Filipovski one-man show mentioned in the last spiski will be extended into February and The Russian Centre will then stage an interesting exhibition of the work of Russian experimental ceramicists. Both the Muscovites are terribly flamboyant. Alyona Mironova's work mixes lace with clay and her phallic heads are also of interest."

End of fragment. No more clues. I wished I had the last spiski, but I did not. I had only this spiski, and not much of it, at that. But I had an address. I put the bit of spiski in my pocket and set off. Cricklewood is my territory: phallic heads do not appear in it unchallenged.

Not that I believed for one moment that that was what was happening; Smiley's person I may not be, but I have picked up a smattering of code along life's literary way, and I know that when one man passes a note to another man informing him that the grey geese are flying tonight, neither is an ornithologist. A spiski to the effect that phallic heads are also of interest must be taken with a pinch of paprika.

303 lay at the northernmost end of the Broadway. You would not know it was Cricklewood at all, were it not that it stands next door to the Cricklewood Hotel, for here the great white way, far from the bright lights of the downtown launderettes and Halal cash 'n' carries, peters out into beige oblongs of anonymous office blocks, not unlike, indeed, the outskirts of Minsk. I parked opposite a dark shopfront with Caucasian Carpets stencilled above it. And, in smaller

letters, Russian Centre. A chain shackled the door-handles, but there was a bell.

Terribly flamboyant was not the phrase. My spiski had led me to expect a giant Cossack in ginger mutton-chops and crossed bandoliers pirouetting towards me on spurred boot-heels, but instead I found myself looking down at a tiny, elderly man in a dusty fur hat, who opened the door a fraction but did not loose the chain. I showed him my spiski. He peered at it, muttered, in a ripe Slav accent, "Filipovski did not come", and made to close the door. "Are the phallic heads here?" I said quickly. It did the trick. He unlocked the chain. I went in. The gloom smelt of shagpile.

"Is downstairs all carpets," he explained, unnecessarily. They were piled floor to ceiling. "Is upstairs exhibition." He shuffled into a ruggy canyon, and vanished.

The exhibition occupied three small rooms. The first contained a few gilded teapots, the second a tall vase, a large ship and a small ship, labelled respectively Tall Vase, Large Ship and Small Ship. I went into the third room; a typed notice identified the work of A. Mironova, but I could see nothing made from lace and clay. All I could see were a few small heads of George Bernard Shaw. They were elongated, true, but with the best will in the world, or at any rate the oddest, you could not term them phallic. It was at this critical point that the glum goblin suddenly reappeared.

"You have seen what you need to see?" he enquired.

"I don't know," I said.

He sighed. "You expected Filipovski. He has not come."

He switched off the lights, and I followed him downstairs, and he took the padlock off again and opened the door. "He may come," said the old Russian. "Do you wish to leave your address?"

"He knows where to find me," I said, and went back into the cold.

Lo, Yonder Waves the Fruitful Palm!

I t is a soft March morning in 1871, and on the drive outside a sturdy London villa, the gravel crunches. Inside, a woman starts, looks up from her davenport, and drops her pen. A sudden vibration shakes her bodice. She knows that crunch. It is three long years since it crunched away, but hardly a day has gone by without her ear's being cocked for its crunching back. She runs to the door, and flings it wide.

"Lawks-a-mercy!" she cries, for popular fiction has been her only consolation during those lonely months, "Mr Forster!"

"Good morning, Mrs Forster," replies her husband, "I am home!"

He enters, removes his topee, bends his sunbleached sideburns to her joyful peck, and places upon their hall table the subject of this chapter.

"And was your expedition fruitful?" enquires Mrs Forster, as her bosom settles.

"Not only fruitful, dearest," he replies, "but seedful, flowerful, and, yes, cormful, too!" (for as well as being a great botanist, he is also a great wag), "and see, I bring you the most illustrious of my trophies!"

Her adoring gaze turns for the first time from his face, towards the hall table. "What is it?" she says.

"It is a potted palm," replies her husband. "Henceforth, no seaside string quartet will ever be the same. It is found only on Lord Howe Island in the Pacific, and since it was found only by me, it is called Howea Forsteriana. Even now, a clipperload is pulling into Tilbury, for the greater glory of English botany. I intend knocking them out at five bob a time, including earthenware tub and watering instructions."

And now, as Mrs Forster swoons, the scene dissolves to another sturdy London villa, another soft March morning, exactly 120 years later, and another great botanist. On this occasion, his is the trembling bosom. He is staring at a polythene cloche tantalizingly fogged by condensation. He is, in apt concord with everything round him, rooted to the spot. Why is he not budging?

To find out, we must, having teleported ourselves this far, now go back six months, to an evening in September when the great botanist went to fill his dustbin, and found his Howea Forsteriana standing beside it. His wife had thrown it out, on the grounds that it was dead. The great botanist brought it back inside, on the grounds that one green frond was still hanging on, and observed to his wife that you wouldn't bin a canary with 90 per cent moult. You would attempt to revive it.

His wife said it was horrible to look at. The botanist, while forced to agree that the item could no longer be classed as decor, maintained that this was no reason to murder it. He had enjoyed a happily symbiotic relationship with the plant for ten years; when he breathed out, it breathed in, and vice-versa. They were mates. If you will not have it in the house, said the botanist, I shall stick it in the garden. At this, his wife selected a sharp snort from her professional repertoire, and pointed out that his moribund friend was a sensitive tropical soul who would not last five minutes out there.

The botanist glared at her for a bit, and slunk off to phone Kew. No chance, Kew corroborated, and went on to tell him more about William Forster than he thought he'd ever need, but there you are, journalism is full of surprises, you never know your luck. Most to the point, they said that Lord Howe Island did not know the meaning of the word frost.

But the great botanist did not know the meaning of the word defeat. In a sheltered southern corner of his garden, he either planted or buried the palm, depending on whether he or his wife was telling it. He then put a polythene cloche over it, leaned a sheet of plate glass against it, and, in due course, watched the snow fall on it.

That is why, this March morning, he cannot budge. He dares not. Could be a corpse underneath. But he is not the great Forster's heir for nothing. He girds his loin; moves the glass; lifts the cloche.

There is a palm-tree there. It has new green stalks, and new green leaves. It has not merely survived the winter, it has thrived on it. This is the Tropic of Cricklewood. The great botanist does not, however, pause to preen. He runs to the dustbin.

They had a mango last night, and some fool threw away the pip.

Blue Serge

I trudged into the Café de la Paix early on Monday morning, because where else was I going to trudge at a time like that? I screwed a Gauloise into the corner of my mouth, because what else was I going to screw into the corner of my mouth, and I asked for a large Scotch, because what else was I going to ask for?

Cosmo, who runs the Café de la Paix, poured it out and put it on the bar beside the large Scotch he had poured for himself, and, as he did so, the ash fell from the Gauloise screwed into the corner of his mouth and on to his pot-belly, a mere nanosecond before my own ash went the same way. We looked at each other, and I hoped against hope that my eyes were as addled as his, and as sunk in their pouches; certainly, I was as unshaven as he was. We unscrewed our Gauloises, we lifted our glasses, we mouthed a silent toast, and we drained them at a gulp, and at the tables behind us a dozen other unshaven, pouch-eyed, pot-bellied, middle-aged men unscrewed their Gauloises, mouthed silent toasts, and drained theirs. While, of course, the jukebox played *Harley Davidson*. What else was it going to play?

For, *par hasard*, I had arrived in France only hours after Serge Gainsbourg had, *par hasard*, departed it. It should be pointed out that the two *hasards* were different, because theirs is a sparse vocabulary, where words have often to box and cox, which is to explain that while I had arrived by chance, Serge had departed through risk.

As he had always been bound to do. If umpteen heart and liver operations have left your torso looking like a zippered *blouson* but you still insist on filling it with 100 Gauloises a day and washing them down with two bottles of Scotch, then the odds grow short, as you reach September, of that moment arriving when the fire brigade axes your door open and discovers you spreadeagled between your last drink and your last dog-end.

Which was precisely what had happened. I did not know this until I walked in from Nice airport and switched on the Sunday evening news to see if anything had happened en route, and learnt that, as far as the news was concerned, only one thing had. The broadcast was exclusively devoted to the passing of Serge Gainsbourg, a single fact, but one copiously and illustriously annotated: François Mitterrand, the president of the republic, said he was desolated, Jack Lang, the minister of culture, said he was stunned, Jacques Chirac, the mayor of Paris, said he could not express his sense of personal loss, and umpteen other members of the great and good jostled for any roving mircophone prepared to pick up their weepy obsequies.

All bloody odd. It was as if, at the death of Jeffrey Bernard (whom God preserve) a red-eyed John Major were to stumble towards the dispatch box, sobbing to the effect that he knew he spoke for the entire House, while up the road a whey-faced footman was simultaneously hanging a bulletin on the Buckingham Palace railings explaining that though Her Majesty was herself too overcome to speak and had gone to lie down for a bit, she wanted, at this grievous time, to send her deepest condolences to all at the Coach and Horses.

For Serge Gainsbourg was not himself a member of the great and good at all, he was a 62-year-old pop singer who rather than go to all the trouble of holding a tune, preferred to croak his indecipherably booze-slurred words through his permanent cigarette, punctuating his public appearances with oaths, insults, threats and obscenities. He had gone to astonishing lengths to make himself France's most famous derelict: his pouches had pouches, his pot pots, his bristles bristles. More: all this unsavoury decay had worked its way on what had itself been pretty horrible to start with. *Joli laid* he had never been, only jolly *laid*.

But jolly laid. That was the key. Gainsbourg was France's premier sex-symbol. Women beat a path to his door on their hands and knees, in the hope of boomps-a-daisy. He stood in that uniquely French tradition of successful gigolos who, in other cultures, would be offered nothing better than tuppence for a cup of tea.

That is why, last Monday, the pot-bellied unshaven of our village convened to mourn his passing and toast his memory. He had given our fantasies credibility. It's more than Robert Redford's ever done.

Your Feet's Too Big

I am growing. Not vertically, laterally. And growing, not swelling: this is not about weight, it is about length. Although I thought it was about weight at first. I thought I had fat feet. I looked at them for a time, and since I couldn't be sure whether or not they had grown fatter, I tried lifting them up to see if they had grown heavier.

It was impossible to tell. Standing on one foot and dangling the other to see if it seems heavier than the last time you did it is a sensible diagnostic course only if you can remember how heavy it was the last time. I do not keep a record of such things. I do keep a record of other things, however, which we shall come to in a bit, but we have to go to Russell & Bromley first, because this harrowing narrative requires me to retrace my steps exactly, especially as those steps were larger on the way back from Russell & Bromley than they were on the way there.

For a couple of weeks prior to the inspection and the weighing, I had been uncomfortable in my shoes. I have four pairs, all pretty old. I do not like buying new shoes: there is the bit where you walk up and down the window outside gazing at the gleaming ranks of these somewhat comic things and vainly attemping to imagine them poking out of the ends of your trousers, there is the bit where you enter and engage in the unsettling intimacy of being unshod by someone you have never met, there is the bit where the shoes come out of their boxes and you limp up and down in one of them, very carefully so as not to crack it and therefore totally unnaturally and therefurtherfore totally uselessly for assessing its comfort, and there is the bit where you go out of the shop carrying the only pair of shoes you hated when you first saw them in the window.

Since all these bits precede the bit where you get them home and try walking about in them the way you normally walk about, only to discover that they seem to be made of teak, you will understand why I hang on to the old ones.

But since all eight had pinched for a fortnight, and since the foot inspection had thrown up nothing pedally untoward, I concluded that for some reason they had all been blighted by shrinkage, and I hobbled off to Russell & Bromley, albeit with a sinking foot.

"Eight-and-a-half," I told Russell, or perhaps Bromley.

A lot of boxes got emptied. A lot of limping got limped. Nothing fitted. It was then that a new bit was added to the other bits, which was the bit where Russell brought a lot of nines out. All the nines fitted. Russell and I agreed that it was a funny old world, and I bought the pair I hated when I saw them in the window, and came home again.

Which was when I remembered that many years ago I had had a pair of brogues made for me by John Lobb, who gave me a sort of blueprint of my foot so that further shoes might be built for me, wherever I was in the world, simply by bunging the blueprint in the post. I dug this out, and discovered that, in 1970, my foot was $10^{1}/_{8}$in long. I took my sock off and my ruler up. My foot was now $10^{3}/_{8}$in long.

A quarter of an inch may not be much after 20 years, but the evidence was that this quarter of an inch had grown in the last fortnight. Do you remember *The Incredible Shrinking Man*? Bloke jumps into an atomic mist of some kind, next thing he knows his trousers have gone baggy and in a short time – literally – after that, he is up to his neck in the shagpile and fending off his cat with a hatpin,

Though I am not a household word where nuclear physicists foregather, it strikes me there might well be a connection here. I might, a couple of weeks back, have stepped into something atomic. My feet could be growing at an extrapolated six inches per annum. In a couple of years' time I shall look like Grock. If a cat doesn't get me (it will be impossible to run away from something feral) and I live out my biblical allotment, my dead feet will be 10ft long. Even allowing for a 6ft grave, I shall project 4ft above the cemetery sod. In order not to appear ridiculous, I shall require a tall hollow tombstone with my feet inside it. If I live to 90, I shall need a cenotaph.

And as for my shoeshop bills, they don't bear thinking about.

We Are Two Cricklewoods, Now!

At the risk of startling those of you unaware that a sentence might be cobbled to include them both, I have to tell you that, like Lord Byron before it, Cricklewood awoke one morning to find itself famous. On exactly the same morning, as a matter of fact, provided you are prepared to discount a gap of 179 years: March 26. Nor, at a guess, would the manner of Cricklewood's waking have been too different from Byron's, since no less common to both than their overnight fame is their custom of tying on a few large ones before turning in.

Especially as, in both cases, March 25 had been an even heavier night than usual, and with good reason: just as Byron had, in 1812, been celebrating the public appearance of *Childe Harold's Pilgrimage*, so Cricklewood had, in 1991, been celebrating the public appearance of *The Pick, The Shovel, and The Open Road*.

Though not a poem but a television film, this too was unquestionably an epic, and likewise picaresque: a tale of other deracinated wanderers upping stakes from green hills far away, backhanding a manly tear, and, murmuring "Adieu, adieu, my native shore!" or at any rate its equivalent contemporary gist, breasting brave the eastward foam. To arrive, in their case, in Cricklewood. And begin shovelling.

For Molly Dineen's fine C4 documentary had taken as its subject the "Green Macs", those sturdy adventurers who have made the long trek from Donegal and Tipperary for the sole purpose of descending into London's vast subterranean Gruyère and digging even more holes in it, in the fond hope that the pavements above will thereby turn to gold. It doesn't happen, but they can handle that. I know this, because we drink together. What, however, they are finding trickier to handle is fame. I know this, because, last Monday night, we watched together.

At first, it was joy to bask and chortle. Just to see the word Cricklewood getting itself nationally networked was enough to bring our cheers rattling the jugs upon the alehouse shelf, even before each glimpse of this beloved spot and that called forth more individuated yells. Here was The Crown, king of pubs, there the Galtymore, queen of ballrooms, and wasn't that McCleary's Coin-Op in the corner of the screen, and Molly Malone's Cafe and Restaurant, and Sheahan's Irish Meat Centre?

Nor were we partisan of anything but place: we spotted the Madena Halal Cash 'n' Carry and loyally we roared aloud; we raised a confraternal glass to Aktar the Chemist; we felt our hearts glow warm on Mr Lee's behalf when the Rainbow Chinese Restaurant found itself, briefly, in a flash of limelight.

And all this, of course, was nothing to the shrieks and cheers for faces known. Nor even faces: a boot was recognized, a digging elbow, a half-glimpsed nose, a half-heard oath, a running donkey-jacket. And so wildly and uncritically enthusiastic was the response to the sheer, wondrous fact of cathode recognition for Cricklewood that every word that anyone said on-screen was itself taken up, tossed about, hooted over, drunk to, and generally celebrated, with no thought of its possible implications.

Until, that is, the morrow morn. Sadder, wiser men, was what, on March 26, I found the Cricklewood Tavern full of; they had not merely woken to fame, they had woken up to it. For it had been borne in upon them that Cricklewood was not made up exclusively of those who applauded the notion of booze and song and vagabondage – at which the film had hinted, in the course of recording the grim labour for which this relaxation was the reward. In short, the good people of Cricklewood, who clearly saw themselves as just that, had not been slow to make known their view that the fame which had just been conferred was not the sort of fame the suburb wanted at all.

Oh dear. Begorrah, possibly. I may just have to speak to someone about shooting a second documentary, showing chartered accountants repotting their azaleas and dental surgeons buffing their Volvos and Conservative councillors sipping Badoit . . .

I should not want the wider world to think that Cricklewood was mad, bad, and dangerous to know.

APRIL

Gnawing Doubts

O ne of Our Men is coming. I may have to kiss him on the lips. Either that, or he has to kiss the squirrel on the lips. I'm not too sure about Mafia protocol. This is my first contract.

I seem to remember that the kiss is called *il colpo di grazia*, though, and that you have to keep your mouth shut afterwards, otherwise you infringe *omertà*, and if you infringe *omertà* you aren't half for it, a lot more kissing goes on, and you end up as part of a flyover.

I have just looked that last sentence through, and I see that it is open to misinterpretation. I should not like you to think I do not intend to keep my mouth shut *during* the kiss as well, as a matter of fact, I hope to get away with the briefest of pecks, I am not a Latin and nor, I would guess, is Our Man, and I see no reason for either of us to go overboard about this, it is simply a formality. We may not even need to involve lips at all. We might get away with the lightest brush of cheeks. This is Cricklewood, not bloody Palermo.

Of course, if it's the squirrel he's supposed to kiss, I don't

187

care one way or another, they can go at it like knives, if they want to.

Were I a heavier sleeper, none of this would have arisen. I should not have awoken at three o'clock on Monday morning and lain there wondering what it was that was scuttling about above my head, and I should not have crawled out of bed, finally, and gone up to the loft with a torch and the thing for turning the stopcock off (nobody has a poker these days, central heating has much to answer for), and I should not, when I switched on the loftlight, have spotted the subject of the hereinabovementioned contract. I did not spot it for long, mind: there was a split-second of mutual identification, during which we both quivered a bit, then it sprang from the joist, shot like a fur bullet through a hole in the Contiboard wall, and vanished into the pipe-cavity. I did not follow, partly because there isn't room in there to swing a thing for turning a stopcock off, but mainly because you never know with squirrels, you hear a lot about post-Chunnel rabies these days, I did not want to come down to breakfast and have people saying: "What's all that foam doing round your mouth, electric shaver bust?'

So I went back to bed. After a while, the scuttling started again.

At 9.30am, I phoned the London Borough of Barnet, and the woman said you mustn't have a squirrel in your loft, once they've found a way in they never leave, and what they do is, they chew the flex off your electric cables, you could have a fire, and did you know that your house insurance policy does not cover this, shall I send somebody round?

"An exterminator?" I said.

"We don't call them that," she said, and I could sense that her lips were pursed in that disapproval which betokens membership of a caring authority. Did Barnet, perhaps, merely bring the squirrels in for counselling, get to the root of their personal problems, set them up in a snug council drey, explain how to apply for supplementary nut benefit?

"You don't kill them, then?" I said.

There was a pause. "Not on the premises," she replied. "Shall I put you through to our man?"

"What we do," said Our Man, "is we bait a trap and we collect the item for disposal later."

"Then you kill it?"

"Definitely." Our Man was not a lip-purser. Our Man was a torpedo. He dealt with items. Could be a squirrel, could be a cockroach, could be The Creature from the Black Lagoon, it made no odds. Rehabilitation was not his bag. If the trap fits . . .

We have made an appointment. Even now, he will be climbing into his long black borough overcoat, tying his white silk borough scarf, taking his ominous borough violin case down from its shelf. I am waiting at the window, staring out into a garden in which the squirrels are happily disporting themselves among the crocuses. I can remember when the kids used to ask me which was Nutkin, but there you go, flex is flex, and house insurance is house insurance, and what are you going to do when the council makes you an offer you can't refuse?

Home and Colonial

On Monday morning, spring suddenly burst upon Cricklewood with the unnatural abandon of a Disney cartoon – you would have sworn *Song of the South* was re-running outside your window, Uncle Remus baritoning *Zip-a-de-dooh-dah* beneath the pastel clouds of blossom while bluebirds twittered around his grizzled poll

189

and Bre'r Fox pursued Bre'r Rabbit across his flapping boots – and I decided that the moment had come for the year's first stroll to Menelik Road.

I do not know why it is called Menelik Road. I have long wondered why this exemplar of suburban gentility should have been named after the sturdy Negus of Abyssinia who in 1896 drove the Italians from his premises, and the most plausible guess is that as the end of the war in neighbouring Sudan brought redundancy to British squaddies, they crossed the frontier to offer the Negus their mercenary services, and following victory, repatriated themselves to Cricklewood to build these trim villas on their spoils; but it remains a guess.

Certainly, Menelik Road has both an Afric and a martial air: the houses have not only unnecessarily sturdy walls to keep out the sun and inappropriate balconies to take advantage of it, they have little turrets and crenellations and embrasures, as if in anticipation of assault. It has often occurred to me that, were one ever called upon to defend Cricklewood to the death, Menelik Road would be the place to take one's stand. The very name has the ring of the honours board: *During the Battle of Menelik Road* (reads the London Gazette citation) *Corporal Coren was gallantly leading the remnants of the 17th/21st Cricklewood Borderers in a spirited counter-attack, when he stopped to look in a pig-bin and an assegai got him. His men carried him into the shade, where his last words were a request to hear Pedro the Fisherman played on the regimental harmonica.*

What drew me to Menelik Road on Monday, however, was not the end but the means. To reach it, it is necessary to negotiate the only country lane in Cricklewood; called Hocroft Walk, it bisects the playing-fields which are Cricklewood's last greenfield site with an avenue of unofficial trees. It is thus the best spot in the parish to take advantage of the rising sap, and accordingly, on Monday morning I plunged into the dappled tunnel, and found it good.

For, that is, about a hundred yards. It was then that I noticed the first empty Volvic bottle. You know Volvic; it is spa water, and it comes in oblong plastic containers, unlike Evian, which comes in cylindrical plastic containers. You could discover this distinction for yourself on Monday by walking five yards further down Hocroft Walk and looking at an empty Evian container. Ten yards on, and there were not only several more of each, but empty Perrier bottles, too. Nothing odd in this, you will say, our filthy environment is full of such jetsam, but the fact is not only that Hocroft Walk has hitherto been free of all litter, but that the litter which last winter had now, for the first time, brought, was exclusively made up of things which had held mineral water. There were no beer-cans, burger-boxes, fag-packets, wine-bottles or chocbar-wrappers, nor any other of the vile detritus we have come to accept as the legacy of the grazing oaf, but then there have never been any of these eyesores in Hocroft Walk, a phenomenon I had always put down to the unique public decorum of the people of Cricklewood.

What had happened? Why had we suddenly been infested with Evian louts? What, indeed, could have possessed such people – clearly neither drunks nor vagabonds – to have so betrayed the mores of the middle-class to which they must have belonged?

I shall never know, for a different answer was about to offer itself. A lateral thinker might have guessed it, but I needed the old gent who, as I skirted the last plastic bottle into Menelik Road, was himself emerging from one of that road's houses and making for Hocroft Walk. He was about 80, but brisk; neat in tweeds, and carrying a black bin-liner. "Just going to do the plastic," he said. "I've done the rest, but you have to take the plastic to a different dump." And off he trotted.

A military man, you would have said. A stickler for bull. One of the old brigade. The sort of chap you'd expect to find in Menelik Road.

The People's Flag is Deepest Blue

I have bought the paint. It is called Prussian Sky, but it is not as militant as it sounds: a bright blue, yes, but an unprovocative one. We are out to persuade, not to incense.

I have not yet bought the placards, though. Much research has to be undertaken before I do, we shall have several meetings on this topic alone, set up a Placard Committee, possibly even a Pole Steering Group. Once, that is, we have decided on the form of procession. If we are going to march on foot, we shall be able to have long poles and large placards, though we shall have to bear in mind that many of our number will be knocking on a bit; too big a placard, too long a pole, and a sudden gust could easily bowl them over or, worse, blow them up against a police horse, and we all know where that could lead, look at Peterloo. Also, several might well be using Zimmer frames, and it is no easy task to lean on the one while waving the other, flailing could result, and that will get us nowhere, except into the back of a white transit, with an Alsatian's jaws clamped on our sleeves.

If we are not marching at all, however, but going for the motorized option, we shall have to have short poles and small placards, to enable them to be poked out of the windows easily. And, of course, as easily brought back in: you do not want to stay up all night painting your placard only to have it come off the end of your little pole in an emergency, such as a police charge or tear gas attack. Furthermore, arthritic members (there could well be a fair percentage) will have to have very small placards indeed; the toll on an octogenarian wrist could be quite severe after half an hour, and the last thing we should want to do is leave a lot of litter about, we are not that kind of person; nor do we need to offer the police any hostages to fortune, God knows what they could trump up, Riotous Littering, perhaps, or Conspiracy to Leave Rubbish All Over the Place, we could be looking at the wrong end of six months' chokey, no fun at all if the court won't let you go privately.

Still more difficult is deciding what to paint on the placards. "No Property Tax Here!" seems a trifle hysterical: we should not wish to appear rabid. "No Property Tax, Please!", on the other hand, is clearly too supplicant. I have of course thought of modifying "Can't Pay, Won't Pay!", but though "Can Pay But Would Rather Not" may have the virtue of honesty, it lacks a certain ring. I have asked around, and the consensus among my neighbours stands at "We Really Feel the Property Tax is a Trifle Unfair, You Know, All Things Considered", but if you put that on a little arthritic placard, the writing is so small as to be virtually illegible, especially as most of the potential support among pavement spectators is likely to be presbyopic, boding the horrifying prospect of their having to crane forward, knocking over police barriers and inviting the zealous truncheon.

Communal songs and chants are another crux. Sweet reasonableness is all very well as a catchword, but the revolutionary spirit is hardly to be stirred by "We Believe We Have a Good Case for Overcoming" or "We Should Prefer Not to be Moved". I have thought long and hard, too, about "Major, Major, Major, Out, Out, Out!", but not only does nobody desire that, they do not want to risk upsetting so nice a chap; the best I could muster, I'm afraid, was "Heseltine, Heseltine, Heseltine, Reconsider, Reconsider, Reconsider!" Try it, however, and you will see that this is a slogan well-nigh impossible to incant once, let alone reiterate during a Long March, especially if a fair proportion of those

193

still bravely hobbling behind you no longer have their own teeth.

Still, I am assured of much solid radical support. Stewards have been offered by the Cricklewood Heterosexuals for Real Suet Campaign Committee, the Hendon Ad Hoc Fair Isle Cardigan Collective is lending us its leaflet printer, the Michael Denison and Dulcie Gray Street Theatre Workshop is considering a kerbside production of *French Without Tears*, and we shall be accompanied by the Hampstead Estate Agents Cooperative Marching Band.

Best of all, I know I can count on my readers, which is why I have written this in the first place. Your suggestions, please, on a placard.

A Better 'Ole

Over the past couple of days, I have seen enough animated busts to last me a lifetime. Not, of course, that I have any idea how long a lifetime lasts, which is why I became involved with the animated busts in the first place. Also a fair number of storied urns.

All the urns, mind, told pretty much the same story, viz, we are standing here on top of someone lying here, may we implore the passing tribute of a sigh? Which, naturally, I offered; the least I could do under the circumstances, since, lucky old me, I was not under anything else.

Not, anyway, for the time being. Time being what it is, however, it is only matter of it before someone will be chiselling urns and busts for me. Though what I'd really prefer is

194

an anchor: I have seen a lot of anchors over the past couple of days, too, and they're very fetching, especially when well-mossed, jauntily tilted, and attached to a symbolically broken chain in permanent dangle; but I imagine you would have to be a dead sailor to qualify. I do not know what a dead hack qualifies for, I did not see any marble typewriters with the keys symbolically wedged into a terminal jam, but I suppose you could ask.

First things first, though, even when it comes to last things, and before the wife and I start flipping through stonemasons' swatches, we have to find a site to put something up over. All right, down under. I introduce my wife, by the way, only because choosing a grave was her idea. She is a practical lady, and when, leafing last Monday through our local rag, she spotted a report that the cost of a Barnet burial plot is to rise from £225 to £270, she read it aloud to me. Not so that we might take instant advantage of this corking deal – though practical, she stops short at viewing a suicide pact as a smart way of saving ninety quid – but as a sly prolegomenon to making me think practically, too. Would it not be sensible to purchase a few feet of diggable sod now, rather than wait to the last minute and be forced to hurtle hither and yon with a coffin on the roof-rack and a shovel in the boot?

The first thing I discovered was that Cricklewood has no graveyard. As an impending rude forefather of the hamlet, I felt this to be a bit stiff, especially as, if you *are* a bit stiff, Barnet can offer you only Hendon Cemetery. I do not want to be part of Hendon: Hendon is not me. I put this to Barnet, and she picked up her map, noted that I lived a mere quarter-mile from Hampstead Cemetery, and asked if I had known anyone in Camden for 25 years. If I did, and they would vouch for me, I could get under Hampstead.

Hampstead is not me, either, but it is less not me, so we went to look at it; a mite uneasily, because though that quarter-mile may be a small step for man, it is a giant step for estate agents, and I should not like posterity to judge

195

that though I could not afford its chic in life, I could not resist it in death.

That said, it is a pleasant spot. Or, rather, several hundred spots of differential pleasantness: choosing a grave is thus much like choosing a house – should it be secluded or convenient, were we after an old characterful bit or a new trim bit, did we want a sunny aspect, a peaceful shade, a view, a tree, a nice stone bench?

You can go barmy. You start wondering what you'll like when you're six feet under it and unlikely to be in a position to like anything. You end up going to look at cemeteries in Kilburn and Hammersmith and Islington and anywhere else a local resident will vouch for your not creating any posthumous trouble, and after a bit you come home again and wonder whether you've missed anything, might there be something beneath a nice yew somewhere, a stream, a lowing herd, a lea?

The upshot is, you can't top Highgate. Highgate was a knockout. Highgate we really wanted to be seen dead in. The trouble with Highgate was that a double plot, 4ft by 6ft 6in, cost £5,000. Unless – and here our charming guide allowed himself a tiny cough – we cared to be buried not side by side, but, er, how should he put it?

Stacked, is how he should put it. 2ft 6in by 6ft 6in, but dug nice and deep, and two of you can get out for a mere £3,120. Since, though, it is also what you get in for, it clearly needs a bit more thought.

Not difficult, once you are clear about the bit more thought it needs.

Pipe Opener

"It isn't a question of how I see you," replied the man opposite me, "it's a question of how *you* see you."

"Not easy," I said. "I'm new to all this."

"The first thing to ask yourself", he said, "is am I straight or bent?" I cleared my throat. "I've never really thought about it," I said.

"We're all either one or the other," he said. "I speak from long experience. Oh, a lot of gentlemen will claim they're a bit of both, it all depends on the mood they're in, and so on and so forth, but when it comes right down to it, they're either straight men or bent men."

I swear that not only is the above verbatim, but that the *verba* concerned were uttered impeccably straight, unbent by wink, nudge or other louche emollient. Now, while it is true that professionals whose careers are fraught with innuendo understandably grow weary at the leers of tyros, they generally smile, albeit wanly, at the obvious, to set others at their ease. Especially if the others are customers. Not this man. This man was serious. His shop was serious. Choosing a pipe was a serious business.

As, mind, it was for me. The purchase of a boy's first pipe is a rite of passage, especially if the boy is 52. Yet more especially if the boy has been, exclusively, a cigarette-smoker for 30 years, because, well before that fork in the nicotine path where the straight men turn one way and the bent another, the crossroads has been negotiated at which

197

fagmen and pipemen part company. They are very different animals, their division bespeaks a world whose poles are Humphrey Bogart and Stanley Baldwin. Quite why I should, at this late stage, have embarked upon the expedition from one to the other, I cannot be certain. Call it a madcap whim.

What was unquestionably certain was that there was more to this than met the teeth. As I gazed at the gleaming racks and the bizarre tags identifying each item, I saw they were not merely individuated personalities but, collectively, an entire masonry. Pipemen doubtless met in blue-wreathed rooms and said things like: "Yes, I can see you're puzzled by my Zulu Pot, and it's true I've been a Bent Diplomat these twenty years, but now the kids have grown up, I rather feel . . ."

"I'll try something straight," I said. "What about this one?"

"I'm not sure you have the chin for a Senior Bulldog," he said. "But you might get away with a Long Chimney." He decased it, and fitted a rubber protective over the stem. "I take it you have your own teeth?"

You will be impressed to hear that it was a bait to which I did not rise. Had this been a less serious shop, I might well have enquired whether they did teeth upstairs for those who did not have their own, and if, while they were at it, they did chins for those determined upon Senior Bulldogs, but I forbore. I put the pipe in and looked in the mirror. My grandfather looked back at me.

"Isn't it a big ageing?" I said. It came out as "Ing bing aing?", but the assistant's ear was clearly long used to the novice bicuspid.

"It has gravity," he countered. He did not need to tell me. It was dragging my head off centre. Filled, it might well confer a serious limp. I took it out and asked to see something lighter. Did you know that the Aluminium Duke was not a nimbler descendant of Wellington, but a Don with a silvery stem? I put it in. I looked like a borough surveyor. I took it out again. "What about that one?"

"A Poker?" he said. He pursed a lip. "Tell me," he

enquired, "do you manufacture a lot of saliva?" He might have been the Queen going round a new factory.

"I've no idea," I said. "How much is a lot?"

"The Poker," he said, "has a broad bore. You may find that it sizzles." I did not intend to. As far as self-image was concerned, just walking in there had brought me a long way from *Casablanca*. Sizzling would take me to the far side of Stanley Baldwin. I pulled myself together, for time was fleeting, and, on an impulse, bought a Horn.

All right, it's a little bit bent. But I think I can handle it.

Radio Fun

"Ah, never can fall from the days that have been, a gleam on the years that shall be!" Well, possibly; on the other hand, Lord Lytton, you never know your luck.

On Sunday night, while the rest of you were frantically measuring the width of your kitchens, filling your stairwells with hollered enquiries about one another's ethnic origins, attempting to remember whether you had more or fewer academic qualifications than John Major, and banging on your teenaged children's bedroom doors in an attempt to ascertain whether they were (a) elsewhere in England, Scotland or Wales, or (b) sharing the room with someone temporarily overnighting (and asking yourself whether, in this event, you should cough loudly, pause, enter, and enquire of said person whether he or she customarily drove to his or her place of employment in a three-wheeled car or a

motor-caravan, and how he or she would describe themselves when he or she got there, e.g., "poultry processor" or
"jig and tool fitter"), I was doing none of these. I had ticked
all my 1991 census boxes and gone, not only elsewhere in
England, Scotland or Wales, but elsewhere in time. I had
teleported myself back 40 years, to the 1951 census.

I had done this, let me quickly say – lest Her Majesty's
enumerator became agitated at one of his quarry's having
slipped the statistical net by means of a black hole in it not
anticipated with a line of little boxes inviting householders
to tick the decade they were currently inhabiting – in the
Paris Theatre, Lower Regent Street, where the BBC was
recording a new episode of *Breakfast with Braden*.

The BBC was not of course doing this to commemorate
the 1951 census, but to commemorate the transmission of
the first *Breakfast with Braden*, with which the 1951 census
fortuitously coincided. It had reconvened the only comedy
gang from radio's golden age to be, happily, still intact, and
one, even more happily, who were instantly to prove capable
not only of performing as shimmeringly as they did yesterday, but of doing it as well as anyone is doing it today – an
assertion you will be able to substantiate for yourselves when
the programme goes out, and when the strange background
susurration you may pick up from your sets will not be static,
but merely the noise of Lord Lytton spinning in his grave
with rage at not having foreseen the thermionic valve.

Remember static? You will, and much else too. You will
hear the first chord of Nat Temple's signature music, and
yesteryear will spring full-blown into your head, as if you
had dunked a madeleine. It will be *Breakfast with Proust*.
You will hear the svelte glottis of announcer Ronald Fletcher
and you will feel again, between finger and thumb, the
Bakelite knob of a walnut Murphy the size of a wardrobe,
and remember twirling it to distinguish the Home Service
from Allouis and Hilversum and Bolzano. You will hear
Benny Lee warble "You're in Kentucky Sure As You're
Born" and you will no less surely be back beside your 1951
Easiwork cabinet where your flaring nostrils will detect the

tang of a Welsh nut in an Ideal boiler (there were no boxes concerning central heating on the 1951 census form) and the reek of rationed rind sizzling on the enamelled gas-stove and, through the gappy single-glazing, the *rus-in-urbis* whiff of the milkman's horse; for this was breakfast-time, then.

You will, furthermore, hear Pearl Carr sing "P.S. I Love You", and it will be no reflection on a voice still girlishly romantic that it will in all probability call up the way unslippered feet stuck to kitchen linoleum or the way tea-leaves used to clog the waste-pipe; just as when, furthermost, you hear the unchanged voices of Bernard Braden and Barbara Kelly, you might recall how your father, who no longer sits behind anything, once sat behind the *Daily Sketch* with nothing visible of him but the overalled arm scribbling on the pools coupon beside his plate according to the *Sketch*'s recommendations, in the days when Accrington Stanley could still be relied upon for an away win.

Fill them in how we may, censuses cannot fill in such things for us, to paint a true picture of cultural change. *Pace* Victor Borge, because it reaches the parts other things cannot reach, only radio can do this.

MAY

The Veiled Lodger

I t is with an unsteady hand that I take up my pen to write words for whose inadequacy to express the singularity of this remarkable case I can do nothing but throw myself upon the indulgence of the reader.

Last Tuesday, I found myself in Baker Street and, it being a little after 4.30pm, in need of some refreshment. As fortune would have it, the doors of the Sherlock Holmes Hotel stood open, affording an enticing prospect, at the further end of the foyer, of young women going about their business with cakestand and teapot. I strode inside, negotiated my passage through a throng of Japanese visitors jabbering before the displays of meerschaum pipes, illustrated undervests, keyrings, and jars of Sherlock Holmes's Raspberry Preserves, and sat down, at last, to peruse a menu requiring a well-nigh impossible choice between Mrs Hudson's Afternoon Tea and Sherlock's Tiffin.

Eschewing the former only because it boasted finger sandwiches – those who recall the incident of the engineer's thumb will not query my apprehension – I was soon tucked into crumpet and teacake, and about to order a lemon fancy when my eye lit upon a handbill on the table beside mine. *The Sherlock Holmes Museum, 221b Baker Street*, it announced, *open until 6pm*. I sprang up, and summoned the waitress.

"Quick!" I cried. "There is not a moment to lose! Even now, I fear we may be too late! I trust you have your service pencil?"

And, scattering a number of Swedes trying on deer-stalkers, I flew.

That 221b lay next door to 237 puzzled me only momentarily: when you have eliminated the impossible, whatever remains, *however improbable*, must be the truth. A card beside the bell read: *Visitors for Mr Holmes and Dr Watson, please ring. Thank you, Mrs Hudson.*

The bell jangled, and a girl of perhaps 20 summers materialized.

"I'm the housekeeper," she said. "It's five pounds."

That it briefly occurred to me to question the nature of the house she was keeping reflects discredit upon me alone: long years in the vilest alleys of the metropolis may corrupt even the worthiest imagination.

"Mrs Hudson?" I enquired. "Temporarily," she said, and led me up a scrofulous staircase to a suite of rooms so diminutive, shabby, and ill-furnished that a deep gloom invaded my spirit. The great detective had clearly earned little from the world to which he had given so much: the tiny parlour contained two rickety tables, one with a jug, plates, and egg-cups upon it, the other supporting a dusty test-tube rack and a schoolboy's microscope, Beside these, a cheap display cabinet revealed a few dented artefacts so pitiable in their modesty that the eye could not forbear a tear; which, at the sight of a beggar's violin leaning, twisted, on the hearthstone, brimmed and fell.

The other room held an old bed hung with a hand-lettered card pleading: *Do not sit on this*. Mrs Hudson pointed at the faded coverlet.

"Look at that!" she muttered. "Can't they read?"

It was the bumprint of a gigantic tourist!

I sighed, and said: "Tell me, who owns this place?"

"Mr Adiniance," replied Mrs Hudson. "He's on the top floor."

"A strange name," I murmured. "Perhaps I might meet him?"

"He doesn't see anyone without an appointment," said Mrs Hudson, "but I could tell him you're here." She went out. I heard her feet upon the boards above. I tiptoed after, and cleared the stairs just as Mrs Hudson emerged, shutting a door behind her. She started.

"I didn't see you," she said.

"That is what you may expect to see," I said, "when I follow you."

"He doesn't want to meet you," she said, and slipped past me.

I looked at the door for a long time, and fought my wild thoughts as long. Holmes's had been an iron constitution; more yet, he had ever plunged deep in arcane sciences to which one dared not give a name. But, stared I never so intently at the spotty doorknob, I could not make myself reach out. Beyond might lie a story for which, like the giant rat of Sumatra, the world was not yet prepared.

Thin Red Line

There's bankruptcy in the air these days. You can taste it on the wind, acrid as zebras. The island teems with busted entrepreneurs sailing out of AGMs on to their ears, stumbling brokenly into courtrooms, shoving black homburgs between themselves and the urgent cameras, stuffing the third set of books into carrier bags before scurrying to private airstrips, or simply banging their heads upon their leather-topped desks for the last bitter time as the smirking bailiffs work their way towards them across the foreclosed Wilton, crating the fittings as they go.

And all the mealy-mouthed opprobrium of the media pours down upon these victims in a withering enfilade of sanctimony and *ben trovato* outrage. When all the time they should be honouring the bankrupt as hero, springing forward with laurel and huzzah as he is hustled through them to his Black Maria, whipping round for his wife and kids and starving polo ponies, and bunging up statues to these buccaneering spirits who dedicated themselves to the chanced arm, but finally fell to the rapped knuckle.

For we are a race that traditionally glorifies failure to the point where – provided it is catastrophic enough – it becomes more honourable than success: ask an Englishman to define heroism, and his eyes will brim at the memory of Captain Scott retreating to Dunkirk at the head of the Light Brigade. So, by that token, why should we forbear even from gumming a humble plaque to the distrained premises of a hero who threw ten million pounds at hazard and went to the wall at 2p in the pound?

I do not, of course, refer to the insignificant busted, the man who wheedles a couple of grand out of NatWest for a lolly-van which he subsequently drives into a ditch the day its insurance runs out, but to the visionary whose silver tongue can cozen a million out of merchant banks greedy to underwrite his scheme for turning Snowdonia into a hypermarket, or extracting plutonium from sleet.

What are such geniuses but seekers after North-west Passages, graves of Prester John, mines of Solomon? What but heroes prepared to leap over the top into fiduciary no man's land, jink through VAT minefields, single-handedly knock out their competitors' pillboxes, vault the Revenue's wire, and zig-zag on regardless, before being cut down, at last, by overwhelming commercial odds.

Especially, as with all true heroes, they are not merely this but also ego-ideals of what we ourselves might be, had we the bottle and initiative. Can there be many of us who are not incipient bankrupts, lured in over our heads, albeit by less extravagant dreams? Are we not all in some form of mundane unheroic hock? For lust of having what should not be had, we take the Golden Road to Carey Street: suppose, tomorrow, our banks, our mortgagees, our credit-card companies, our HP brokers, all decided to reclaim everything, immediately – would there be a majority of us able to flip open the wallet and see them off? The only difference between us and the Great Fallen is that we are the conscript bankers to their Napoleons and Rommels, we are the rank-and-file who have been persuaded to borrow the Queen's shilling, and we shall scramble through somehow to save our skins, survive only because we're not worth bothering about, while the generals are busted at drum-head courts-martial, stripped of their rank and insignia, and required to break their bright swords across their knees.

Would that I could summon the nerve to put someone else's money where my mouth is! Go literally for broke, scrounge a million or two by some glib stratagem, to found a chain of unisex fast-muesli bars, or market a range of chic self-packing luggage, or launch an Alice Faye satellite channel into the tellysphere, which would let me ride the heady, fragile crest for a glorious year or so before the whole heroic enterprise came to pieces in the Receiver's hands.

It will not happen. When it comes to livelihood, I know the frontiers of my courage. The typewriter is in my wife's name.

Fat Chance

I engage today's nugatory theme for no better reason than that life has a way of chucking up pleasing circularities; from which it follows that we should not turn a blind eye to the displeasing ones. They are there to stop us from getting cocky. They are there to remind us that what shapes our ends is not invariably divine.

I have been attempting to avoid lunch this week. Gent's tailoring being the time-consuming inconvenience it is, bespoke alterations to what lay beneath seemed a sensible alternative to standing around getting chalked and struggling to decipher what a man with a mouthful of pins thought about the Conservative leadership.

The only way to avoid lunch is to get out of the way; find something else to preoccupy body and mind. I managed well enough for the first three days – a game of tennis, a Waterstone browse, an embedding of geraniums – and on the fourth I set off, at noon, for the Nehru exhibition at the V & A. Now, when I go to the V & A, I always park outside the PLO headquarters in Clareville Grove. The meter there is usually free, doubtless because parkers think it is the most dangerous place in London to leave a car. They have not given enough thought to the possibility that it might be the safest.

I arrived at 12.30, with a circumspect pocketful of 10p coins, and pulled in alongside a nice new parking meter. It was nice and new because, in the two months since I had last parked there, it had been converted to 20p coins, of which I proved to have an unpocketful. The policeman stationed outside the PLO had only one. I bought 15 minutes, and went into the Bar Escoba, next door.

They did not give change for parking meters, they gave beer.

A pint is hardly lunch.

My change contained one 20p.

But a ham sandwich is hardly lunch, either, especially if you just eat the ham; and you do get two 20p pieces in the change. After you have just eaten the ham, it occurs to you that a brisk walk to the V & A would almost certainly burn up a couple of titchy bits of bread.

"Nick of time," said the copper, when I got back to the meter and put in the three coins to see off the risen penalty flag and give myself 45 new minutes. Not enough for a museumload of Indian exquisitries.

"They've installed this computerized till," said the woman at Peter Dominic, next door to the Escoba. "It doesn't do No Sale."

It does Sale, though. Since I did not wish to walk round the V & A with a bottle of gin, I bought a packet of Phileas Fogg tortilla chips, and got 15 minutes in change. Tortilla chips are hardly lunch. They're gone in a flash. So is a Mars Bar, which gets you a full half hour at the kiosk opposite Peter Dominic.

"You're not supposed to feed it," said the copper.

"I'm allowed two hours," I said. "I've still got 40 minutes to go."

I needed them. I needed that much time striding round the V & A to work off what was hardly lunch. I jogged back into Brompton Road; was there nowhere that didn't sell food?

Yes. There was Hani Dajani. It sold pharmacy, it did not sell phood. I went in and scoured the shelves for something that gave quarters-of-an-hour out of a £. I did not want to lug a lot of pharmacy round the V & A. It was then that I spotted the weighing machine. It cost 20p.

211

I put a quid on the counter and asked for change to weigh myself. They gave me a 50p and five 10ps. The machine did not take 20p coins, it took two tens.

Since I had demanded the change in order to weigh myself, face demanded that that was what I did. It was an electronic machine. It had buttons. You punched in your sex and height, and it gave you a print-out. The print-out read: "Your weight is 13 stones 2lb. The approximate ideal weight for a male of 5 feet 9 inches is 11 stones 9lb. Overweight? Ask the pharmacist for advice."

The pharmacist was Andrew. I know this, because they called him up from the basement. When Andrew arrived, I asked his advice.

"Try eating less," said Andrew.

Thus Far and No Father

She looked terrific. There are not many girls who can get away with a purple velour hat at nine in the morning. Bold, unquestionably, but still demure enough to cheat that boldness of brazen threat: a paragon, you would have said, of confident innocence. I drew my chair closer, leaned towards her, and, because she seemed a trifle pale, adjusted her colouring a touch. I brought up the peaches and enriched the cream.

This, as he sprang through the scenery behind her, had a rather unfortunate effect upon Mr Robert Kilroy-Silk. Already tanned to the standards of a sun-bed brochure and doubtless further enhanced with enough layers of BBC mahogany panstick to ensure the morning swoon of the nation's more vulnerable matrons, he now assumed the patina of a Sheraton sideboard. He looked like Geronimo. Indeed, as he paused beside the girl in the purple hat, I was reminded of nothing so much as that moment when the Sioux brave leaps upon the lurching buckboard and advances on the settler's cowering daughter until such time as the *Winchester ex machina* intervenes to settle his hash.

I did not have a rifle. All I had was a remote control, but I brought Robert down, if only by a shade or two. It was the least a daddy could do.

Especially as he had encouraged his daughter to expose herself to danger in the first place. Not, it must be said in his defence, that he had not already reassured himself of her ability to handle the wicked world beyond their simple Cricklewood burrow: when, on Monday morning, Victoria announced that the *Kilroy* programme had telephoned to invite her to appear the following day, her caring daddy immediately asked her what it was about. When she replied that it was about a hundred quid, he concluded that she seemed to need protection from the Wild Wood no longer. Even when, pressed, she mumbled off-handedly that the theme of the discussion was to be fatherhood, he did not demur; rather, he preened himself that the programme's researchers had thrown up so peerless an exemplar of a daddy's work. Get in there, Victoria, was his first thought, and show them what you are made of, for thereby (was his second thought) they will appreciate whom you were made by.

Thus it was that I woke her betimes on Tuesday, gave her a hot breakfast and, with the injunction to be sure to run straight to grandmother's studio, deliver her basket of opinions and run straight home again, saw her off. I may have blown my nose into my pinny; certainly I waved. It was the least a daddy could do.

An hour later I switched on and there she was. There they all were, three dozen eager faces, hot to chat: young faces, old faces, female, male, ambiguous, a typical cross-section, in short, of people who want to run round to Shepherd's Bush and get things off their chests.

Things about fatherhood? Not entirely. Considerably unentirely, in fact. For the topic, when announced, turned out not to be daddies at all, but their redundancy. Virgin birth was the *plat du jour*, AID for women attracted only by ends, not by means. Syringehood was what they were going to talk about.

But I was not fazed. As Kilroy-Silk cried havoc and let slip the dogs of bigotry, I could see Victoria's face amid the shrieking mêlée of barrack-room philosophers honking this half-baked extremism and that, and the face shone like a good deed in a naughty world. Let proponents rant of sexual colonialism, let opponents bang on about original sin, let any crackpot chapter, verse, or statistic be speciously adduced, it mattered not, for these were mere adults, marching their jackboots beneath the banners of principle alone. But any second now a little child would lead them. That was why she was there. She would point out the difficulties of climbing upon a syringe's knee. At last the lens swung towards her, the microphone nudged. "I have an open mind on this," began Victoria, "and . . ."

How she ended, who can say? You, perhaps, if you were watching. For me the room swam. *An open mind?* On *daddies?* I bit my knuckle, but felt nothing; he was not wrong about serpent's teeth. Would she truly as lief I had been a test tube?

"How was I?" she said when, later, I opened the front door.

"Terrific," I said. It was the least a daddy could do.

214

Shelf Life

If all our knowledge is ourselves to know, then those who like nothing more than to curl up in front of a roaring fire with Alexander Pope can count themselves fortunate indeed that the tiny wag was born too soon to push a trolley round Boots. Had he done so, his creative ambitions would never have reached the point at which the universe's deeper truths were to be addressed; emerging once more upon the pavement of Finchley Road with his bulging bags of toilet requisites, he would have scuttled home to write not the *Essay on Man* but the *Essay on Sensitive Teeth*. This he might well have followed up, a deliberative year or so later, with the *Essay on Brittle Hair*, subsequently crowning what would by then have become a less than illustrious career with the *Essay on Delicate Skin* and its companion epic, the *Essay on Serious Perspiration*.

For these days, who among us can find the time to get to know himself philosophically, when just getting to know himself physically grows more and more difficult with every passing marketing fad? I went into Boots last Saturday at ten o'clock, and when I came out again at half-past, all that I knew about myself was that I now knew less. Daily, my body was becoming more and more imponderable; here I was, in middle life, at that point when I should be addressing such questions as why are we all here? where are we all going? and what's it all about? and so on, and I did not have even a working knowledge of the thing depending from my hat.

The Boots trip was a major expedition. We had suddenly run out of everything simultaneously, and while our various bathroom cabinets were normally restocked on a spasmodic basis by this member of the family or that, the present occasion called for a comprehensive foray if we were not to become pariahs: self-love and social are the same, as Pope himself said, even though he didn't know he was talking about deodorant and bath-gel.

Of both of which there are, of course, umpteen varieties. As many as there are different shampoos, soaps, shaving-creams, toothpastes and, after these have done their primary work, secondary things to splash over, gargle with, massage in, squirt between, rub on, apply under, and so forth, until there is not a preposition left unused. Now, I had not hitherto paid much attention to these items when, as I mentioned, a solo bar or tube or bottle had to be summarily snatched for a specific emergency, but this time was different: my remit was totally to replenish, and, furthermore, bulk-buying seemed sensible. To this end, I began reading labels. It was a grave error.

I counted 17 sorts of hair, but not only did I not know the categories into which the rest of the family's fell, I did not even know mine. What is dull? What is brittle? How lifeless is lifeless, how unmanageable unmanageable? Is greasy oilier than oily, or vice-versa? Did it need revitalizing, or merely conditioning? Where did its body lie on the national bodiness scale? I finally grabbed a dozen bottles of something pH-balanced with silk protein and enriching moisturizers, which may very well raise barley on my scalp come spring, only because time was pressing and I needed toothpaste.

But did I have sensitive teeth? How could I know? Might my teeth be not merely indifferent, but callous? Brutal even? And how tender does a gum have to be before it requires .05 per cent of an additive bent on sorting it out? How discoloured should discoloured be before special care must be taken when applying something to undiscolour it?

The deodorant shelf needed to know if I had serious perspiration. What is it? Do your boots fill constantly from your upper cataracts? If mine is frivolous perspiration and I spray serious stuff on, will my pores snap shut and my impermeable body slowly swell with incarcerated sweat? As for bath-gel and shaving-cream, the choice of both depended on whether the skin was or wasn't delicate. What is mine? If it's crude, will my dirt and bristles refuse to budge? How can I know? What shall I buy? Whom should I ask?

What mighty contests rise from trivial things!

A Fight For Love and Glory

Of all the departure lounges in all the airports in all the world, she had to walk into mine. As a matter of fact, she had to run into mine; but even then she was too late. What made her too late was that I had run into it just before her.

This was not the Casablanca airstrip in 1941, mind, this was Heathrow in 1991; but while the difference between them might seem considerable, you must remember this: an airport is still an airport, as time goes by. Which is to say that, just as Bogart's Lockheed Electra was overbooked then, so my Boeing 747 was overbooked now. I did not, though, know that it was, when I arrived to check in – until the check-in advised me to stir my stumps, because the flight had been overbooked, and the last call had been called, and if I were to start mucking about in, say, Duty Free, musing perhaps on the relative appeals of Glenfiddich and Smirnoff, then I might well find myself nudged out of the winner's enclosure.

217

I therefore galloped straight to the departure lounge, got processed, and collapsed into a chair.

A scant minute later, she fetched up, panting, at the gate: one of those young women on whom panting has always looked much better than it does on me. It could, however, not help her now. Chagrin suffused the attendant's face, you could see that if it were up to him he would gladly have pushed her to Nice in a wheelbarrow, but there was nothing he could do.

Spectating this, my heart, so recently preoccupied with banging itself against my hurtling ribs, now changed gear into a more poignant (though no less risky) rhythm. It melted. For she did not rant, or curse, or stamp her foot, as you or I would have done; she sighed, she shrugged, she smiled a brief wan smile. She was, in short, behaving not so much with decorum as with resignation. She was clearly someone to whom this was but the last in a long line of tragic setbacks. She walked slowly to the window; she stared silently at the plane she could not board. Rarely can there have been a sadder stare, nor one more fraught with imponderable sub-text. It came from beneath a low-brimmed yellow hat, but I shall not describe her further, since those romantic men among my readers whose empathy I wish to enlist will prefer to dispose beneath that hat such features as they personally deem optimum. I shall say only that as far as the *quality* of the features was concerned, imagine something that would leave Ingrid Bergman at the post, and you will not go far wrong.

Was she fleeing from? To? Both? Were the VAT-SS on her lissom heels, the DVLC, *Reader's Digest*? Might Victor Laszlo be in the lounge behind me, disguised beneath a ginger wig, not daring to contact her? But before I could mull further, I was hauled from musing by an announcement from the desk: "This flight has been overbooked, and we have someone who urgently needs to get to Nice. Is there any passenger who would be prepared to take a slightly later flight, via Geneva?

At this, there was a lot of coughing and hemming and

hawing, but no more than that. A couple of minutes passed, racking me: I did not want to get a later flight via Geneva, I was not even wearing a trenchcoat or a trilby, but you will never know how much I wanted to walk across to the sad-faced girl and growl: "I'm not good at being noble. But it doesn't take much to see that the problems of two little people don't amount to a hill of beans in this crazy world. Some day you'll understand that; not now. Here's looking at you, kid." And give her my boarding card.

I rose from my chair, slowly. Too slowly, by a nanosecond: for, as my knees straightened, the desk came back on to its microphone: "If any passenger is prepared to take the later flight," it said, having obviously had a bit of a think, "British Airways would be prepared to offer Denied-Boarding Compensation of £100."

You would not believe how easy it is to round up the usual suspects; just as they had sprinted to the gate to get on to the plane, so now they sprinted to the gate to get off it. I felt their slipstream tug my hair.

I did not, of course, enter the contest. That is not how I wished her to remember me. I did not want her, some day, to understand that what the problems of two little people in this crazy world amounted to was a hundred quid.